THE HEAVENLY OCTAVE

A STUDY OF THE BEATITUDES

F. W. BOREHAM

THE ABINGDON PRESS

NEW YORK   CINCINNATI   CHICAGO

BOREHAM
THE HEAVENLY OCTAVE

Copyright, 1936, by
F. W. BOREHAM

Printed in the United States of America

CONTENTS

Contents

"Blessed are ye, when men shall revile you, and persecute you, and shall say all manner of evil against you falsely, for my sake."

"Rejoice, and be exceeding glad: for great is your reward in heaven: for so persecuted they the prophets which were before you."

CHAPTER I
THE PRINCELY POOR

THE world has its own idea of blessedness. Blessed is the man who is always right. Blessed is the man who is satisfied with himself. Blessed is the man who is strong. Blessed is the man who rules. Blessed is the man who is rich. Blessed is the man who is popular. Blessed is the man who enjoys life. These are the beatitudes of sight and this present world. It comes with a shock and opens a new realm of thought that not one of these men entered Jesus' mind when he treated of blessedness.

—Ian Maclaren.

WHEN Master James Hutcheson lay dying, he turned to Master Andrew Turner, who sat at his bedside, and made a last confession.

"For upward of forty years, Andrew," he said, "I have been preaching to men the assurances and promises of the gospel; yet there is but one promise in all the Bible that I dare now make use of. It is this: *'Blessed are the poor in spirit, for theirs is the kingdom of heaven.'* "

—Wodrow's Analecta.

CHAPTER I

THE PRINCELY POOR

"Blessed are the poor in spirit: for theirs is the kingdom of heaven."

I

AMONG the stirring records of those rude times when the white settlements in the vast American forests were subject to constant invasion at the hands of the Indians, I find a story which furnishes me with an excellent starting point for my present study. It was a sultry day; the little meetinghouse was crowded, and, to render conditions more tolerable, the doors and windows stood wide open. While the meeting was in progress, the red men emerged silently from the woods and crept like snakes across the grassy plot that surrounded the building. Their chief, the terrible Black Eagle, was at their head. Gliding toward the open door, he was to observe the disposition of those within, and, at the right moment, to give the signal for the impending massacre. But, as he paused beside the portal, he heard a solemn voice—subdued, reverent, impressive—reading some strange and wondrous words. The sentences to which he listened in astonishment were these:

"Blessed are the poor in spirit: for theirs is the kingdom of heaven.

9

"Blessed are they that mourn: for they shall be comforted.

"Blessed are the meek: for they shall inherit the earth.

"Blessed are they which do hunger and thirst after righteousness: for they shall be filled.

"Blessed are the merciful: for they shall obtain mercy.

"Blessed are the pure in heart: for they shall see God.

"Blessed are the peacemakers: for they shall be called the children of God.

"Blessed are they which are persecuted for righteousness' sake: for theirs is the kingdom of heaven.

"Blessed are ye, when men shall revile you, and persecute you, and shall say all manner of evil against you falsely, for my sake.

"Rejoice and be exceeding glad: for great is your reward in heaven: for so persecuted they the prophets which were before you."

As stealthily as he had come, Black Eagle crept away. "If *these* be the laws of the palefaces," he said, "let them live and teach the red men the same holy doctrine!"

II

Blessed! Blessed! Blessed! Nothing could have been more exquisitely meet and fitting than that the earthly ministry of the Prince of Glory should open in a perfect galaxy of benisons and blessings, a cataract of beatitudes and benedictions. Moses preached the first Sermon on the Mount to the accompaniment of thunders and lightnings, and that sermon had left the world under a terrifying condemnation. Jesus, his great antitype, appears; he too ascends the mountain height, the multitudes eagerly following him. And when, being set, he

opens his mouth to speak, he proves that grace has
been poured into his lips by letting his first word be
a word of benediction: *Blessed! Blessed! Blessed!*

III

Now, the old world had its own ideas about happiness or blessedness. That old world was divided
into two classes—those, on the one hand, who, looking at everything superficially, lived lives of gaiety,
frivolity, and dissipation; and those, on the other
hand, who gave themselves up to the study of philosophy. But the supreme aim of both was the same.
How to be happy?—*that* was the insistent inquiry.
Each of these sections had its own conceptions, its
own ideals, its own beatitudes; and both were
amazed and astounded when Christ solved the com-
plex problem by pointing out an unsuspected, un-
dreamed-of way to blessedness—a way at which
they had neither of them guessed. The materialists
said, as the materialists still say, *"Blessed are the
rich!"* Jesus said, *"Blessed are the poor in spirit."*
They said, *"Blessed are the merry!"* Jesus replied,
"Blessed are the mourners." They said, *"Blessed
are the mighty!"* Jesus answered, *"Blessed are the
meek."*

That philosophy was no more successful is evident from the fact that, although no fewer than
eighty guesses had been made as to the secret of happiness, there was still no word suggesting true humility in the language either of the Romans or the

Greeks. That way—the way of modesty and meekness and tears—had never crept into their imaginations. "It is a pathetic reflection," Mr. Gladstone once observed to John Morley, "that while humility is the sovereign grace of Christianity, the Greeks had no symbol in their language to denote it. Every word akin to it has in it some element of meanness, feebleness, or contempt." Then, suddenly and startlingly, as a rebuke to the world, as a beacon to philosophy, and as a watchword to his followers, Jesus unfolded the mystic secret. *"Blessed are the poor in spirit,"* he said, *"for theirs is the kingdom of heaven."*

IV

Now, there has always been inextricable confusion in the minds of men as to the relationship in which Poverty and Wealth stand to Happiness. Occasionally we hear, *"Blessed are the rich;"* anon somebody contends, *"Blessed are the poor."* And Christ, in this very first beatitude, settles the difficulty forever and forever.

1. The World has always shouted, *"Blessed are the rich!"* And it is of no use stopping our ears to the impressive testimony that can be advanced in support of that proposition. For surely wealth, properly manipulated and discreetly administered, should carry a man a long way toward the attainment of happiness. And yet actual results conclusively prove that the affirmation requires some

qualification. Many wealthy men have been cease-lessly oppressed by anxiety, disquietude, and unrest. The very investment and security of their wealth have been an intolerable burden to them; and a long string of well-known names could be cited to prove that, among such men, depression has been common, despair frequent, suicide occasional, and madness not unknown.

2. But then the Church, singularly enough, took up the selfsame cry, proclaiming in effect, *"Blessed are the rich!"* For centuries the Church sold, for money, her pardons, indulgences, and other spiritual favors; and, if these were blessings, it followed that the wealthiest were in a position to be most fully blessed. Indeed, one of the earliest factors in the Reformation was the opening of the eyes of the poor to the anomalous fact that, since they could afford neither to purchase the deliverance of their friends and relatives from purgatory, nor even to obtain their own personal pardon, the teaching of the Church placed the rich on a much more favorable plane of blessedness than the poor could ever hope to reach. The beatitude of the World, *"Blessed are the rich!"* became the beatitude of the Church; and the Church, by adopting it, stultified herself.

3. Then came the reaction. It set in first of all in the Church. Like a pendulum, knowing no mean, but always swinging from extreme to extreme, the Church suddenly proclaimed, *"Blessed are the poor!"* One of the first signs of a change was the rise, as

early as the twelfth century, of various orders of Mendicant Friars, among whom none was more famous than Francis d'Assisi, who, taking a vow of poverty, clothed himself in rags and courted starvation. Thus these bewildered and perplexed friars rushed from one pole to the other, and, abandoning their faith in the blessedness of wealth, became inordinately enamored of the blessedness of poverty. And multitudes followed, obeyed, and almost worshiped them.

4. The World soon adopted the same strange cry. Every sane school of political economy sets itself to decrease the selfishness of the rich, to correct the vices of the poor, and to lead both rich and poor to a fuller appreciation of their mutual obligations the one to the other. But there is a spurious imitation of this admirable ideal. Taking for their watchword, "Down with everything that's up, and up with everything that's down!" these unhappy theorists seek to foster in one section of the community a burning hatred of the other. And by crying perpetually, *"Cursed be the rich!"* they cry by implication, *"Blessed be the poor!"*

With two incisive words Jesus swept these distorted ideas into oblivion. Blessed, he said, are neither rich nor poor unless they be rich in faith and poor in spirit; while with *such* wealth and *such* poverty, blessedness may be the portion of either or both. He knew that poverty in spirit might reside as well in a palace as in a hovel; as well beneath a crown as within a pauper's garb. He knew that a bundle of inflamed and virulent pride might as easily be garbed in rags and tatters as in ermine robes, and that haughtiness may as often be seen in a thatched cottage as in a turreted castle.

The ancients treasured with a chuckle a story concerning the behavior of Diogenes when that eccentric cynic called upon Plato the philosopher. Plato was, of course, as much the superior of his visitor in ability as in modesty. Finding Plato pleasantly housed, Diogenes stamped upon the luxurious rugs at his feet, and exclaimed, "Thus do I trample under foot the pride of Plato." Plato was too good and too great a man to take much notice at the time, but shortly afterward he returned the visit. Finding Diogenes living in ostentatious poverty, he languidly observed that he could see the pride of Diogenes peeping through the holes in the carpets! It is possible for the poor to be proud of his poverty, for the devout to be proud of his piety, for the prayerful to be proud of his supplications, for the idolater to be proud of his obeisance, for the fasting to be proud of his fasts, for the donor to be proud of his gifts, for the penitent to be proud of his penitence, for the lowly to be proud of his lowliness. It is, Coleridge avers, the devil's darling sin:

> "The devil did grin, for his darling sin
>   Is the pride that apes humility."

With one lancetlike word, Jesus probed beneath all

externals and outward appearances, beneath all
visible wealth and showy poverty, beneath all mere
forms and ceremonies, beneath all our ostentatious
goings and givings, beneath all looks and profes-
sions, beneath all self-advertising words and works.
Penetrating to the very quick and marrow of our
inner, truer, secret selves, he said, "Blessed are the
poor in *spirit;* for *theirs* is the kingdom of heaven"!

V

In his classical essay on *The Everlasting Yea,*
Carlyle has an unforgettable passage in which he
shows that the principle embedded in this first beatitude is inherent in the very nature of things. The
man who whines and whimpers because he is not
happy is obviously a man who regards himself as entitled to happiness—a proud and smugly self-satis-
fied man. "Foolish soul!" exclaims Carlyle, "what
Act of Legislature ordained that *thou* shouldst be
happy? A little while ago thou hadst no right to be
at all!" The man who cherishes an inflated estimate
of his own worth will fail to find happiness in the
midst of the most superabundant luxury, while the
man who feels that he is unworthy of the most micro-
scopic mercies will find a banquet in every crust of
bread, a sacrament in every drop of water, and in
every common goblet will see the Holy Grail. There
is, says Thomas à Kempis, perpetual peace with the
humble; but the proud and the covetous are never
at rest.

When, some years ago, the government irrigators were at work in Southern India, they were troubled by one man, a native farmer, who resisted their efforts on the ground that his land was quite hopeless.

"It is hard, dry, incapable of verdure," he said, "is it possible that it can be watered?"

"Yes," replied the officials, "it can be made rich and fruitful *if it lies low enough!*"

There stands the crucial test! He who walks open-eyed through a wheatfield, notices that it is the drooping ears that are heavy with grain; the stems that hold their heads erect are the empty and worthless ones.

It is always so. Our choicest blessings invariably come to us by descending; our richest benefits come by going downward. We stoop to conquer. The farmer bows his face toward the earth both to sow the seed and to reap the harvest; the miner goes below for the precious things of the earth; the loveliest streams flow along the lowliest valleys; the sweetest flowers flourish in the shadiest dells.

> "The saint that wears Heaven's brightest crown
>   In deepest adoration bends;
> The weight of glory bows him down,
>   The most when most his soul ascends;
> Nearest the throne itself must be
> The footstool of humility."

Marcus Quintilanus remarks of his contemporaries that they would doubtless have become most

excellent scholars had they not been so fully per-
suaded of their own scholarship. "He is the wisest
man," says Plato, "who knows himself to be very
ill qualified for the attainment of wisdom." When
Dr. Andrew Bonar was visiting Mr. Moody at
Northfield, the two were walking together one morning when they met a band of students.

"We've been holding an all-night prayer meeting,"
exclaimed one of their number; "see how our faces
shine!"

Turning to him with a quiet smile and a wise
shake of the head, Doctor Bonar quoted a text:

" 'Moses *wist not* that the skin of his face did
shine,' " he said; and the students understood.

VI

I like to think that the word that introduces each
of the Beatitudes is wonderfully rich in historical
associations. Christ's word "Blessed" is an infinitely
lovelier word than our word "happy." Our "happy"
stands related to "hap," "luck," "chance": it is a
gambler's paradise. But the "Blessed" of the Beatitudes is suggestive of natural fruitfulness; it stands
related to the roses round my lawn, to the corn in
yonder valleys and to the autumnal harvest of the
orchard. It has to do with joys that arise spon-
taneously and inevitably from certain fixed conditions. It is the word "Macaria," a name that was
once given to the Island of Cyprus because that
island was said to be so fertile as to be able to pro-

duce upon its own shores everything that its inhabitants could either require or desire. Such is the blessedness of the poor in spirit. The kingdom of heaven—the only true Macaria—is theirs; and, when they at last finish their long fight with self and sin, they shall inherit that happy land where all their chastened appetites shall be fully gratified and all their purified cravings be abundantly appeased.

Well may Sextus Rufus hint that Cyprus, the Isle of Macaria, famous for its fertility and wealth, presented a constant temptation to the Romans; they lusted to seize upon it and make so rich a prize their very own. The wonder is that the kingdom of heaven—the brighter, grander, fairer Macaria—does not entice all earth's knightliest spirits to venture along the lowly track that winds its way through the Valley of Humiliation in quest of such abounding and abiding felicity. Blessed are the lowly and the contrite, for the true Macaria shall be theirs! *"Blessed are the poor in spirit: for theirs is the kingdom of heaven."* It was the King of the Kingdom who said it; and, depend upon it, he knows the laws by which his happy subjects win their glorious victories and gain their glittering crowns.

CHAPTER II
THE HAPPY MOURNER

THIS Valley of Humiliation is the best and most fruitful stretch of country in all these parts. It is fertile ground, and, as you see, consisteth much in meadows. Behold how green the valley is; also how beautiful with lilies! And the pilgrims espied a boy keeping his father's sheep and singing the while, "He that is down needs fear no fall."

Then said their guide, "Do you hear him? I will dare to say that this boy lives a merrier life, and wears more of that herb called heartsease in his bosom, than he that is clad in silk and velvet."

And Mercy marveled at the effect of the valley upon her spirits. Nowhere else had she felt so well. She spoke of it to Mr. Greatheart, and his experience was akin to hers. "I have gone through this valley many a time," he said, "and never was better than when here." And he went on to say that most of the pilgrims whom he had escorted through the valley had said the same.

"I love to be in quiet places like this," Mercy added. "Methinks one may here, without much molestation, be thinking what he was, whence he came, what he has done, and to what his King has called him. Here one may think and break at heart, and may melt in one's spirit until one's eyes become like the fish-pools of Heshbon."

—John Bunyan.

CHAPTER II

THE HAPPY MOURNER

"Blessed are they that mourn: for they shall be comforted."

I

"Blessed are they that mourn!" It is a hard saying; it falls strangely on our ears; we listen in bewilderment, groping vainly for its cryptic meaning. Christianity has always been exposed to the most lamentable misunderstanding and misinterpretation. Those who are its professed exponents have differed sharply in their application of its truths. Some, for example, have found in religion the secret of a light heart, a smiling face, a lilting voice, a blitheness bordering upon gaiety, while others, construing it as a call to austerity and melancholy, have incarcerated themselves in the dismal seclusion of cell and cloister. To one or other of these interpretations this second beatitude lends itself. *Blessed are they that mourn!* It is either the doleful creed of one whose gloomy soul finds its poor joys among the draperies of the dead, or else it is the glad evangel of One who can irradiate earth's deepest darkness, who can uplift those who are bowed down, and who can impart to stricken souls a celestial joy that shall make hallowed smiles to sparkle through the mourner's tears. The fact is that the second beatitude is one of

those abysmal profundities of human speech that a mature experience alone can adequately interpret. Dr. A. M. Fairbairn paints three pictures. The *first* is the picture of a blithe young soul, full of laughter, full of sunshine, full of song. Go to this glad, lightsome spirit and say, *"Blessed are they that mourn!"* The words will seem like the incomprehensible speech of some weird and distant world: the countenance will take on an expression of amazement and incredulity. The *second* picture depicts a man who has been tortured by grief and crushed by heavy losses. His spirit writhes in the dust. Sorrow has soured and embittered him: his soul is in revolt. Go to him and say, *"Blessed are they that mourn!"* The words will mock his suffering; they will act like brine on smarting wounds; to him *blessedness* and *mourning* are not only sharply antagonistic; they are hopelessly irreconcilable. The *third* picture presents to our gaze one who has known the joyousness of the first and the bitterness of the second. "There has been love and loss; vigorous youth or sweet maidenhood lies far behind; the hour of grief with its dull stupor is overpast; calm has come and the nature has emerged from its sorrows richer, more conscious of the infinite within and its kinship with the infinite without." In this case the words that seem so incredible to the sunlit soul in the *first* picture, and so cruelly incomprehensible to the rebellious spirit in the *second,* have been interpreted by the tense realities of an abysmal and illuminating experi-

ence. The eyes, cleansed by weeping, have obtained
a clearer vision of life's profound mystery and beneficent discipline. The subject of this *third* picture
k ·ows the secret of the mourner's blessedness.

That is precisely the Master's meaning. We love
the cloudless hours; yet we love still more the days
when snowy clouds fleck the sky—clouds that, irradiated by the westering sun, become a gorgeous
pageant of topaz and gold. We love the summer
sunshine, yet we love the sweetness of the garden
after rain. We love the exquisite rapture of spring,
yet, but for wintertime, we should never know the
beauty of the crocus. We like the course of true love
to run smooth, yet sweethearts tell us that there is a
delicious ecstasy in making-up. Health is never so
precious as when it returns to us after the long
agony of fever and of pain. In the same way, we
love the sorrowless and tearless days; and yet life
teaches us to love the days when, our souls having
been bowed down in deep humiliation, and our
cheeks made the channels of scalding tears, the tender
benediction of the mourner's beatitude has stolen
into our hearts.

"There is a joy that cometh after sorrow,
    Of hope surrendered, not of hope fulfilled;
A joy that looketh not upon tomorrow,
    But calmly on a tempest that is stilled.

"A joy which lives not now in wild excesses,
    Nor in the happy life of love secure;
But in the unerring strength the heart possesses,
    Of conflicts won while learning to endure.

"A joy there is, in sacrifice secluded;
  A life subdued, from will and passion free;
'Tis not the joy which over Eden brooded;
  But that which triumphed in Gethsemane."

Only those who have experienced that chastened bliss know the true significance of the second beatitude.

II

"Blessed are they that mourn!" It is the glory of the gospel of Jesus that it stoops to the lowliest, bringing the boon of happiness to the hearts that need it most. The blessedness of the world is for the sorrowless, the joyous, the gay; it has no beatitude for the broken and the contrite. Nor can philosophy help. It stands afar off with folded hands, soliloquizing about the brevity of human life, the brittleness of earthly hopes, and the certainty of moral retribution. But it has no goblet of gladness, no boon of blessedness to give.

Indeed, philosophy not only demonstrated its own pitiful inability to find the road to happiness; it went further and affirmed positively that, however and wherever blessedness was to be found, it was certainly not for the poor and the sorrowing. Aristotle solemnly and emphatically declared that there was no way of making life worth living for slaves, because they were the mere tools of their masters; nor for those who were diseased, because nature had doomed them to misery; nor for paupers, because they were too poor to be happy; nor for those who died young, because they had not been long enough in the world to attain it. Philosophy was wandering blindly, wearily, over the bleak and wind-swept moors of human experience, searching frantically after the road to blessedness, yet with its back turned upon the only true way. Jesus came at last and pointed out that way, and multitudes marveled when he exclaimed, *"Blessed are the poor in spirit!"* *"Blessed are they that mourn!"* The words fell strangely on the world's ears; yet the experience of the ages has proved their vindication.

III

"Blessed are they that mourn!" the Saviour says; and I think that I begin to understand him. "Blessed are those who *feel!*" he seems to say. The tendency is to become insensitive. We get used to things. Our susceptibilities become seared. The doctor, who nearly fainted at his first operation, learns in time to look upon pain without emotion. The minister is so much among the sorrowing and the bereaved that he is in peril of regarding the tears of the mourner with professional nonchalance. He takes them for granted. It is not easy under such conditions to keep the spirit fresh and the heart tender. *Blessed are they that mourn!* Mourning implies a soft, copious, heartfelt grief—a grief that has broken all restraint and finds relief in welcome floods of tears. There is all the difference in the world between a keen, cutting wind with just a dash

of rain in it, and a warm tropical shower.   There is just the same difference between the stiff and formal expression of our sympathy and the deep and heartfelt sorrow that is the earnest and surety of real blessedness.

Unless we are constantly on our guard against it, we are all in danger of being drawn into the horrible vortex of insensibility.   A wise man will include among his supplications the impassioned prayer of *De Profundis*.

> "Out from the mist, the mist, I cry—
> Let not my soul in numbness die!
> My life is furled in every limb,
> And my existence groweth dim.
> My senses all like weapons rust,
> And lie disused in endless dust.
> I may not love, I may not hate;
> Slowly I feel my life abate.
>
> "O would there were a Heaven to hear!
> O would there were a hell to fear!
> Ah, welcome fire, eternal fire,
> To burn forever, and not tire!
> Better Ixion's whirling wheel,
> And still at any cost to feel!
> Dear Son of God, in mercy give
> My soul to flame, but let me live!"

Ulysses Androvaldus remarks that a dove is so afraid of a hawk that one feather of that bird will paralyze all its powers.   I have seen a horse thrown into paroxysms of terror on scenting the beasts in a passing menagerie.   Most of us learn to treat with equanimity the things that we should hate and dread.

It is a great art to preserve one's capacity for emotion unblunted to the end.

IV

A brilliant young minister who once occupied my Mosgiel pulpit preached a particularly eloquent and forceful sermon on this strange beatitude; and I had the rare felicity of sitting reverently among his hearers. The discourse of that morning is indelibly imprinted on my memory. Its main contention was that the mourning to which the Master referred was *spiritual* mourning, not mourning for the loss of friends. "Blessed," he said, "are they that mourn over the multitude of their inward depravities and besetting sins! Blessed are they that mourn the paucity of their spiritual attainments! Blessed are they that mourn the tardiness of their progress in the divine life!" We ought not to need, this young preacher reminded us, we ought not to need any special and singular manifestation of the divine comfort when we sorrow over the loss of those we love. For two reasons. (1) The departure of our friends should be contemplated and expected: death is so natural, so universal, so inevitable: we should train ourselves to regard our beloved as flowers that cannot bloom for long. "I begat him mortal!" was the reply of Anaxagoras, the Ionic philosopher, when informed of the death of his son, the devastating news of which was expected to overwhelm him. (2) Our faith in God, our assurance of immortality, and our knowledge of the felicity of the departed should satisfy our hearts, rendering us independent of any special and personal administration of the divine consolation.

At the time I thought this young minister's exposition singularly telling; but, in thinking it over since, I have wondered whether it covered all the ground. The very brevity of the Bible's shortest text has given it an emphasis that has appealed to us all. *Jesus wept!* I have never in my life attended a funeral without pointing out that, since *he* wept, there can be nothing weak or wicked or faithless in our human tears. He made us what we are—quivering bundles of emotion, creatures that cling fondly and tenaciously to one another. He made us what we are—made us in his own image. And, having made us what we are, and made us in his own image, he knows the wrench and the heartbreak. He sympathized; he understood; and so he wept. Is no work of grace effected by such tender tears?

V

And yet I recognize that there was some justice in the contention of the young preacher to whom I listened with such interest that day. The mourning of which he spoke so eloquently is one of the most spacious and most fruitful facts of life. The mourner of whom he was particularly thinking—the mourner who mourns the corruption and depravity of his own heart—may find a foretaste of the blessedness of the beatitude in the very fact that he mourns. He is troubled because his faith is so small, his love for Christ so meager, his zeal for the kingdom of God so slight. Let him felicitate himself on the fact that he has been given grace to recognize and deplore these defects. A thousand times worse would be his case were he unmoved by his lamentable shortcomings. The climax of spiritual tragedy is reached when the prodigal settles happily down in the far country, perfectly at home with his swine and perfectly satisfied with his husks.

We are citizens of a good world—the best of all possible worlds—a world in which it is a luxury to live. And yet no man of open eyes and thoughtful mind can dwell here without realizing at times that there must needs be a limit to our laughter and our song. There are times when all who treasure the interests of the kingdom of God sit in sackcloth and cover their heads with ashes. Every reminder of defilement within, every stifled sob of suffering without, every outbreak of disaster and calamity around, causes the tear to start and the chastened heart to beat to a more solemn measure. Yet even such pangs carry with them their own reward.

A man mourns his sins. The memory of his iniquities is grievous unto him; the burden of them is intolerable. He is appalled at the thought that he has dared to insult a holy, just, and gracious God. Neither the loss of heaven nor the fear of hell troubles him so much as the enormity of his own audacity in violating the grace of the Most High. Such mourning is extremely bitter. Yet only the man who has tasted that cup of woe can experience the rapture of the divine forgiveness, the joy of reconciliation.

A man mourns his spiritual poverty. He thinks of the love, the faith, the devotion demanded of him by the unutterable love of Christ; and, as he ponders his slender attainments, he grieves unfeignedly. He is aware that his heart should be a temple of holy thoughts and noble desires; he is conscious that it is only comparable to a cage of unclean birds. But, even while he bemoans his unspirituality, his spirituality is being intensified; his very mourning deepens his devotion; his grief fortifies his faith; his warm tears inflame his attachment to his Saviour, and, as a result of his lamentation, the very desert, whose dustiness he deplores, bursts into beauty and blossoms like the rose.

A man mourns the waywardness and callousness of his fellow men. Like W. C. Burns, in Glasgow, he hears day by day "the tramp, tramp, tramp of the Christless." It appalls him. He is concerned for his generation, and, like his Lord, he weeps over his Jerusalem. As a natural corollary, he bewails the apparent futility of his own feeble efforts to help, to rescue, and to save. But such mourning, like rain on mown grass, revives and refreshes all that is best in him. He is one of those who, sowing in tears, shall reap in joy. For *"he that goeth forth and*

*weepeth, bearing precious seed, shall doubtless come
again with rejoicing, bringing his sheaves with him."*

VI

"Blessed are they that mourn!" It is one of life's
strange happinesses. At first blush, the beatitude
appears to be a contradiction in terms, an insoluble
enigma, an inexplicable paradox. "Happy is the
mourner!" If he be happy, how can he mourn? and,
if he sincerely mourn, how can genuine happiness be
his? Yet it is sublimely possible! To those who, at
noonday, walk in green pastures and by still waters,
the sky is an unstudded vault of blue; but to those
who, from the abysmal depths of a mine, look up
through the long shaft at the same sky, it is at that
same hour bespangled with sparkling stars. The
purity of the lily is never so pronounced as when
seen against a dark background; the deep bass notes
give verve and grandeur to the song; long absence
lends wondrous luster to the twinkling lights of
home. Only the painracked know the blissful tranquillity of painlessness; only the warrior can fully
appreciate the rapture of triumph; only the watcher
through the midnight hours knows how to welcome
the dawn; and, similarly, only the mourner can enjoy
true blessedness.

"Were there no night we could not read the stars;
  The heavens would turn into a blinding glare;
Freedom best seen is through the prison bars;
  And rough seas make the haven passing fair.

    We cannot measure joys but by their loss;
        When blessings fade away, we see them then;
    Our richest clusters grow around the cross,
        And in the nighttime angels sing to men."

"Wherefore," says Chrysostom, "if thou wouldst be comforted, mourn; and think not this a dark saying, for when God comforts, then, though sorrows come upon thee by thousands like snowflakes, thou shalt surmount them all!"'

In the middle of the nineteenth century a young minister visited Dundee. He was oppressed by the fact that, in spite of diligent study and conscientious labor, his work was not flourishing. He had been reading about Robert Murray M'Cheyne, and he felt that he should like to visit the scene of that extraordinary man's seraphic ministry. Mr. M'Cheyne had recently died at the age of thirty; yet, before dying, he had moved Scotland to its very depths. What was the secret of his amazing influence? The young minister came to Saint Peter's. The old sexton who had served under M'Cheyne was still there. He reverently led the youthful inquirer into the vestry, and pointed to some of M'Cheyne's books still lying on the table.

"Sit down here," said the sexton, motioning his visitor to the chair in which M'Cheyne had so often sat.

"Now, put your elbows on the table! That was the way Mr. M'Cheyne used to do!" The visitor obeyed.

"Now, put your face in your hands!"

The visitor did so.

"Now *let the tears flow!* That was the way Mr. M'Cheyne used to do!"

The sexton led his guest to the pulpit; and gave him a fresh series of instructions.

"Put your elbows down into the pulpit!"

He put his elbows down.

"Now put your face in your hands!"

He did so.

"Now *let the tears flow!* That was the way Mr. M'Cheyne used to do!"

Yes, *that* was the way; and those who today read the story of M'Cheyne's fruitful and abounding ministry will find in it the best possible illustration of the principle embedded in the second beatitude.

CHAPTER III

HEIRS OF THE EARTH

"O Son of Man—thy name by choice—
 Our hope, our joy, our life,
Make us like thee, whose gentle voice
 Was never heard in strife.

"Holy and harmless, undefiled,
 On earth thou wert alone;
Come from the depths of heaven, a child,
 To make the lost thine own.

"To be a glory in our night,
 And bring us from above,
The way heaven's children live, all bright
 With self-forgetting love.

"In all things like thy brethren made,
 O teach us how to be
With meekness, gentleness, arrayed,
 In all things like to thee."
                               —*George Macdonald.*

I READ in the Scriptures the praises of meekness. But when I see a man meek or patient of injury through tameness, or insensibility, or want of self-respect, passively gentle, meek through constitution or fear, I look on him with feelings very different from veneration. It is the meekness of principle: it is mildness replete with energy; it is the forbearance of a man who feels a wrong, but who curbs anger, who though injured resolves to be just, who voluntarily remembers that his foe is a man and a brother, who dreads to surrender himself to his passions, who in the moment of provocation subjects himself to reason and religion, and who holds fast to the great truth, that the noblest victory over a foe is to disarm and subdue him by equity and kindness—it is this meekness which I venerate, and which seems to me one of the divinest virtues. It is moral power, the strength of virtuous purpose, pervading meekness which gives it all its title to respect.—*Channing.*

CHAPTER III

HEIRS OF THE EARTH

"Blessed are the meek: for they shall inherit the earth."

I

THE Beatitudes sum up, in a melodious octave of epigrams, the ponderous contents of a thousand volumes of practical morality. And yet the Beatitudes themselves can be condensed into a single sentence. *Blessedness,* the Saviour seems to say, *consists in character.* It lies, not in thinking something, nor in saying something, nor in doing something, but in *being* something. *Blessed are the poor in spirit! Blessed are they that mourn! Blessed are the meek!* The *first* beatitude sets forth the beautiful modesty of the heart that has been operated upon by the divine grace—*"Blessed are the poor in spirit."* The *second* beatitude denotes the *heavenward* expression of that lowliness—*"Blessed are they that mourn."* And now the *third* beatitude has to do with the *earthward* manifestation of that lowliness—*"Blessed are the meek: for they shall inherit the earth."*

Blessedness consists in character! Anything short of this is a species of hypocrisy. And hypocrisy may assume either of two radically different forms. It may be the hypocrisy of the man who, like Uriah

Heep, pretends to be meek in order that he may inherit the earth.

"I am the 'umblest person going, Master Copperfield," explained the oily Uriah, "the 'umblest person going, let the other be where he may. My mother is likewise a very 'umble person. My father's calling was 'umble. We live in an 'umble abode, Master Copperfield. But we have much to be thankful for, oh, so much to be thankful for!"

And so on. Uriah was everlastingly airing his humility; but in reality he was assuming this nauseous pose in order that he might worm himself into a position of authority and power. He vaguely felt that, in the long run, the meek inherit the earth, so he garbed himself in a counterfeit meekness in the hope that he might obtain that vast inheritance by guile.

This is the *first* of the two forms that hypocrisy assumes. The *second* differs radically from it. It is the hypocrisy of the man who, from the purest motives, sincerely tries to *act* meekly in order that he may have a share in the meek man's spiritual blessedness.

The *first* is unspeakably vicious, the *second* is almost virtuous; and yet both are hypocritical, for the one places pretending, and the other performing, in place of being. The one vital truth emphasized by the Beatitudes, differently applied and differently illustrated by each, but pointedly taught by all, is that true religion consists, not in assuming a rôle, nor in playing a part, nor in choosing a style of conduct, but in living a new life.

The Beatitudes therefore embody the very heart of the everlasting gospel. For how can I live the new life except by way of the new birth? How can I acquire the graces that entitle me to these wealthy benedictions except by becoming a new creation in Christ Jesus? I read these Beatitudes, and, as I do so, I become aware of the obduracy, the selfishness and the pride of my own heart. That terrible discovery drives me to my knees in shame and contrition. Looking up through my tears, I behold the wonder of the cross, and hear, from the lips of the Crucified, His *Blessed, Blessed, Blessed!* And so the Beatitudes prove themselves a group of celestial evangelists, stripping me of all self-satisfaction and leading me to life eternal.

II

We are slow to learn the deepest truths of the kingdom of God, and therefore, with infinite consideration and patience, they are communicated to us, not by way of abstract propositions, but by way of object lessons. Heaven condescends to the simplicity and artistry of kindergarten. Both the Old Testament and the New contain one character who, for meekness, far outshines all his colleagues and contemporaries. *"Now the man Moses was very meek above all the men which were upon the face of the earth."* And Moses continued the meekest man who ever trod the earth until *He* appeared who could say in all humility, *"I am meek and lowly of heart."* And these two—the pattern of meekness exhibited by the Old Testament, and the pattern of meekness exhibited by the New Testament—are brought together in the music of that sublime minstrelsy with which the Bible closes. *"They sing,"* we are told, *"the song of Moses the servant of God and the song of the Lamb."* I used to marvel at that strange conjunction—the song of Moses and the Lamb—but the third beatitude sheds a flood of light upon the mystery.

I hear men speak of meekness as though it were a disposition of the mind, an inherited quality, a matter of temperament, a thing almost entirely constitutional. A meek person is supposed to be a somewhat sparkless and spineless individual—quiet, placid, sluggish, imperturbable, and easy-going. The assumption is absurd upon the face of it. For, if the meek are the heirs of the earth, and if meekness be an inborn temper or propensity, then it follows that the blessedness of the beatitude and the heritage of the earth are to be enjoyed only by those who bring into the world at birth a certain hereditary disposition.

We have but to turn back to our Old-Testament model in order to shatter this fallacy to fragments. Moses was of all men most meek. Yet look at this! In his early manhood he comes suddenly upon a scene that makes his blood boil. An Egyptian slave-driver is lashing a downtrodden Hebrew slave—one of his own kinsmen. It is too much for Moses; and in a few minutes the sand is crimson with Egyptian blood. Does that tragic deed look as though Moses were naturally of a meek disposition? Moses, the young man, a murderer; Moses, the old man, the meekest on earth! Explain the incongruity! The two situations can only be harmonized by a study of the secret history of the intervening stages. First of all, there were long, long years of loneliness away at the back of the desert. Then, during the illustrious public career that followed, there were long, long years of crushing responsibility and of heart-breaking disappointment—years in which life was lived in the constant glare of the limelight. And only those who have thought their way into the spiritual fellowship of that earlier phase, and into the searching discipline of that later experience, can appreciate the softening, ripening, mellowing process that so gradually evolved. By means of all that he saw and all that he suffered, Moses learned to curb the powerful passions that, in his early life, controlled him. He did not extinguish the flaming zeal that slew the Egyptian; but he chained it, harnessed it to lofty ends and stripped it of its savagery.

It is absurd to deplore the possession of a fiery temper. The temper of Moses was, to the end of his days, one of the secrets of his strength. Aaron and the idolaters trembled when, in a fit of holy wrath, Moses broke the two tables in pieces at the foot of the mount. And, turning from the Old-Testament model to the New, we have a vision of Jesus, the meekest of all, who, in his righteous indignation, overthrew the tables of the money-changers and the seats of them that sold doves, and, with a scourge of small cords, drove the cattle from the temple precincts. It is a fine thing to own a dog, provided he does not seize your brother's throat and lick the burglar's hand; it is a good thing to possess a spirited horse, so long as it remains your own prerogative to determine the place and the pace of each journey; it is a good thing to own a gun, so long as it is entirely subject to the cunning of your hand; and, similarly, it is a good thing to possess a temper that feels deeply and acutely and keenly, provided that you have it in complete subjection. The very word "meekness," one authority assures me, is the word used by the Greeks to describe a colt which had been broken in and harnessed. It was once careering wildly over the waste: but now it is disciplined for service. Its strength is not reduced; but its real value has been developed. The souls that, through the ages, have been the deliverers of Israel, have been the meekest of men—calm men, sensitive men, strong men—not doves, but eagles; not timid hares, but lions with eyes of fire and all their mighty forces under magnificent control.

Meekness is therefore a sign, not of pusillanimous weakness, but of splendid strength. Many a man

avows himself a follower of the meek and lowly
Jesus; and the world, pitying his piety, accounts him
spoiled. His refusal to be infuriated under rebuke is
mistaken for lack of spirit; he is regarded as a weak-
ling when, being reviled, he reviles not again. In
point of fact, it would be the easiest thing possible
for him to lose his temper, to rave and stamp and
swear, to strike the well-earned blow, to return
insult for insult. He shows a more imposing
strength by avoiding such an unseemly display. The
light of heaven is on his face, but the fires of hell
burn in his breast; God alone knows the awful
struggle proceeding within. Would it be strength
to yield to his baser self, to utter the word that
trembles on his tongue, to strike the blow for which
his fist is automatically clenched? Or is it strength
to hold the fiendish passions under, to return a smile
for a frown, a blessing for a curse? By his impetu-
ous murder of the Egyptian, Moses manifested his
own lamentable weakness; going away into the
desert, he returned strong in the leonine strength of
the divine meekness, leading his passions in chains
to be exhibited only when the exalted occasion re-
quired.

III

*"Blessed are the meek: for they shall inherit the
earth."* The words appear incongruous. If the
Master had said, *"Blessed are the meek, for they
shall inherit the kingdom of heaven,"* or if he had

said, *"Blessed are the masterful, for they shall inherit the earth,"* we could have understood it. But the *meek* . . . and the *earth!* And yet, on second thoughts, it is clear that the beatitude, as he expressed it, enshrines the actual truth. The meek inherit the earth. We discover every day of our lives that, even in this world, it is not the most pushing and self-assertive who succeed. We select for our friends the most retiring, the most modest, the most unassuming: we do not fall in love with those who violently thrust themselves upon our notice. Those men are chosen for the high places of the earth who are wise and capable and competent; not those who are forever blowing their own trumpets and singing their own praises. David is constantly being called from the sheepfold to the throne in preference to his bigger, prouder brothers. It is the quiet, meek, unobtrusive force that tells in the end. "The gentle dawn will master the blackest night; the soft-treading spring will quell the storms of the winter." Modesty often triumphs over might; and, as Aesop's fable has shown, the soft sunshine effects what the blustering wind failed to accomplish.

The meek inherit the earth. Goodness pays. It came to pass that a quarrel arose between Abraham's herdmen and Lot's herdmen. And Abraham, the elder, said unto Lot, *"Let there be no strife between us or between our servants. Is not the whole land before thee? If thou wilt take the left hand, then I will go to the right, or, if thou depart to the right*

hand, then I will go to the left." Lot chose the
wealthier land; and it looked as if Abraham's meekness and magnanimity had been his impoverishment.
But, later on, when Abraham looked down upon the
land of Lot, and saw that *"the smoke of the country went up as the smoke of a furnace,"* and that Lot
and his household were flying for their lives from
the smoldering ruins, he understood. In the long
run, as Miss Wilcox sings:

> "In the long run, fame finds the deserving man.
>   The lucky wight may prosper for a day,
> But in good time true merit leads the van,
>   And vain pretense, unnoticed, goes its way.
> There is no Chance, no Destiny, no Fate,
> But Fortune smiles on those who work and wait,
>   In the long run."

And, as surely as the morning follows the night, in
the long run the meek inherit the earth.

IV

The earth! *The meek shall inherit the earth!*
Some of the translators, I see, prefer to use another
word. *"The meek shall inherit the land,"* they
render it. And, in that rendering, they see a further
reference to Moses. For Moses, all his meekness
notwithstanding, failed to inherit the land. He was
buried within sight of it. After maintaining a meek
and quiet spirit for more than forty years, after
earning for himself the reputation of being *meek
above all the men which were upon the face of the*

earth, Moses forgot himself once more toward the
hour of his sunset.   The old nature—the nature that
slew the Egyptian—broke its chains; the spirit of
Moses rose in fierce revolt: and, by way of retribution, he was forbidden to enter the land of his desire.

Whe-efore let no ship reckon her perils past until
she is safely anchored in the port; let no runner
reckon the race won until the tape has been breasted;
let no man relax the fervor of his pilgrimage till he
is well within the gates of the Celestial City.   Moses
was *meek above all the men which were upon the
face of the earth,* but his meekness collapsed under a
sudden strain toward the end.   *Let him that thinketh
he standeth take heed lest he fall.*   That is the ad-
monitory undertone that, like a deep diapason, rises
from this third beatitude.

CHAPTER IV
THE DELICIOUS HUNGER

WHEN Laura Bridgman, deprived alike of hearing and of sight, was a small inmate of Doctor Howe's Asylum for the Blind at Boston, her teacher one day made some reference to *the soul*.

A look of bewilderment overspread the girl's face and she slowly spelled out on her fingers the question, "What is *the soul?*"

"The soul," replied Doctor Howe, in the complicated language used in dealing with blind mutes, "the soul is that which thinks and feels and hopes!"

A look of rare discernment mantled the blind girl's face.

"And is it," she immediately inquired with eager fingers, "is it that *which aches so?*"

CHAPTER IV

THE DELICIOUS HUNGER

"Blessed are they which do hunger and thirst after righteousness: for they shall be filled."

I

For some hours I had been sitting with my book beside the fire. Then, overcome by drowsiness, I lowered the volume to my knee and let my eyelids drop. And, presto! before I knew what had happened, I was admiring a wondrous city, a city beautiful for situation, the joy of the whole earth. It was a city four-square and was surrounded by a wall great and high. Peeping through one of the gates I saw golden streets and glittering turrets, graceful gardens and silvery streams. The faces of the citizens were radiant with a calm and holy ecstasy; and as I stood, captivated by the vision of so much beauty and so much gladness, I caught the strains of sacred music and of joyous praise. Recovering from my astonishment, I asked the name of this enchanting place and was told that the city was known to the younger people as *The City of Happiness* and to the older people as *The City of Blessedness*, but that the two titles were synonymous; their meaning was the same. The city was the home of laughter and music, of love and helpfulness, of unbroken tranquillity and of deep content.

And I saw, as I walked around the city, that it had eight gates—one at each corner and one in the center of each wall. Each gate was of pure gold; and over each gate was a marble mosaic into which a motto had been worked, the letters formed of precious stones. And I noticed that all the gates were of the same size—*all but one.* For the great Western Gate was two or three times as broad and as high as the other gates; and the traffic at *that* gate was immensely heavier than the traffic at any of the others. So great, indeed, was the congestion at the Western Gate that I could not, for some time, get near it. And, although I saw that the mosaic over the archway was much larger, and its lettering much bolder and brighter, I could not, at the distance at which I at first found myself, make out precisely what that inscription was.

II

The words inscribed over the other gates I read with ease. Above the keystone of the first gate that I approached—the gate at the Southeast corner—I made out the words: *Blessed are the poor in spirit;* and those who entered by that portal were told that theirs was the kingdom of heaven. Over the next gate—the gate in the center of the Southern wall—I read: *Blessed are they that mourn;* and I saw that the eyes of those who passed under that archway were swollen with much weeping and many were still wet with tears; but I noticed that, as they entered the city, they were immediately and strangely comforted.

And over the next gate—the gate at the Southwest corner—were engraved the words: *Blessed are the meek;* and, to their unspeakable astonishment, the title deeds of the whole earth were presented to those who entered the city through that portal. What had they done, these modest people asked in their perplexity, what had they done to deserve a prize so princely? But no explanation was offered them, or, if it was, it was uttered in tones so low that I was unable to catch it. With their faces irradiated by a joyous surprise, these heirs and heiresses passed from my sight into the city.

And this brought me to the great gate in the center of the Western wall, the gate at which the concourse was so dense that I could not read the glittering letters on the immense mosaic, huge as those letters were. My first impulse was to take my place in the throng, and thus, in time, to approach the gate and decipher the shining legend over its portal. But, I reasoned with myself, as I let my second thoughts assert themselves, if I adopt that course, there can be no retreat. How, in face of the enormous pressure behind me, shall I be able to retrace my steps? If once I become entangled in this seething mass of humanity, I must allow myself to be swept through the great gate into the city. And, once I have entered the city, I asked myself, how shall I be able to discover the mottoes that stand inscribed above the gates that I have not yet visited? And so I decided to continue my pilgrimage to those other gates, and to return to this one later.

And I saw that the next gate—the gate at the Northwest corner—was for the *Merciful*. And the next—the gate in the center of the Northern wall —was for the *Pure in Heart*. And the next—the gate at the Northeast corner—was for the *Peacemakers*. And the last—the gate facing the East— the gate generally known as the Martyrs' Gate—was for those who had been *persecuted for righteousness' sake*. This brought me back to the point from which I started. I had completed the circuit of the city. So I resolved to return to the great central gate—the gate facing the West—the gate at which I had been prevented by the density of the crowd from reading the inscription on the wall.

And it was while I was making my way back to the Western gate that I discovered one of the reasons for the congestion at that entrance. For I noticed that, from each of the other gates, a steady stream of people was turning sadly away. I saw thousands of pilgrims going from gate to gate, eager to enter the City of Blessedness, but finding no gate through which they were entitled to pass. They feared they were not sufficiently poor in spirit to enter the first; they had never sufficiently lamented their shortcomings and besetments to entitle them to enter the mourner's gate; and they trembled when they thought how far they were from being meek.

Then, passing the jostling crowd at the center gate, they looked at the *fifth*. "Alas!" they cried, "we are not merciful, although we dearly long to be!" And at the *sixth* they said: "We are not yet pure in heart; but oh, how we yearn after such snow-white purity!" And when they read the inscription over the *seventh* gate they said, "No, we are not peacemakers; but we should love to be!" And at the last—the Martyrs' Gate—they again turned away disconsolate. They had never dared the lions or the rack or the stake for their Saviour's sake: what right had they to enter there? And then it flashed upon me that the vast concourse at the great gate in the center of the Western wall was largely composed of these streams of disappointed people who had felt themselves disqualified for admission at the other gates.

III

With this new thought occupying all my mind I determined to approach a group of travel-stained pilgrims who, with sad and downcast faces, were wearily turning from the Martyrs' Gate.

"We have come from afar," they explained, "that we may enter the City of Blessedness and enjoy its restful felicity. But, alas, there seems to be no gate by which we are entitled to enter. We are not poor in spirit, much as we should like to be. We have not mourned our shameful transgressions and inward pollutions as bitterly as we should have done; and, although we wistfully covet the grace of meekness, we are far from possessing it. We have been to all the gates—at least, to all but one—and there nowhere seems to be a gate to welcome us."

"And why," I inquired, "have you left one gate untried?"

"It was the great central gate, the gate on the West," they explained. "We thought to approach it, but could not for the press. So we decided to try these other gates before joining the multitude at that one. We propose to make our way now to the principal gate; but our hearts are heavy and we have little hope. Since all these gates exclude us, it is scarcely likely that we shall find a welcome at that one."

"But see," I said, pointing to the Martyrs' Gate from which they had just come, "very few people seem to enter by this gate: the number of martyrs is evidently extremely small: let us go and ask the keeper of the gate if he can tell us what the words are that stand inscribed upon the large mosaic over the great gate on the West! We shall then be able to decide as to whether it is worth our while to join the immense throng that is surging into the city through that archway."

To my delight, they heartily adopted my suggestion. The keeper at the Martyrs' Gate—oppressed, as it seemed to me, by his loneliness—was only too eager to enter into conversation and impart the information that we sought.

"You see," he observed, "there are great numbers of people who turn sorrowfully away from these seven small gates. They go, for example, to the gate at the Southeast corner—the gate for the *Poor in Spirit*—and, when they read the inscription, they feel that they are not sufficiently lowly, and so they turn sadly away. Or they go to the gate on the North—the gate for the *Pure in Heart*—and they shrink from attempting to enter: they are too conscious of their own defilement. And so they begin to fancy that the City of Blessedness is not for them."

I saw my companions glancing meaningly and hopefully at one another at hearing their plight described with such exactitude.

"But," the keeper at the Martyrs' Gate continued, "it is one of the fundamental principles of the City of Blessedness that, just as there is sin in the appetite for sin, so there is grace in the desire for grace. There is lowliness in the longing for lowliness; there is meekness in the yearning for meekness; there is purity in the craving for purity. And so a gateway —the largest gateway of all—has been placed in the center of the Western wall for all who, pitifully conscious of their own imperfections, nevertheless covet, and covet passionately, the virtues that they know they lack."

I noticed that by this time the faces of the pilgrims were wreathed in gratified smiles. Their eyes sparkled with a new hope; they had forgotten their weariness; and I confess that my own heart was glad.

IV

Impatient to be gone, we thanked the keeper of the Martyrs' Gate for the priceless information he had vouchsafed; and, with feet that almost danced, we set off for the Western gate. Joining the multitude, we slowly pressed our way toward the archway, and, as we drew close to the entrance, we read the great words on the glittering mosaic—words that infected our eyes with their gleam and sparkle:

> BLESSED ARE THEY THAT HUNGER
>
> AND THIRST AFTER RIGHTEOUSNESS

And so, with glad hearts and shining faces, we passed into the City Beautiful. And, with the joy of it, I awoke.

V

My book, which happened to be a *Life of Abraham Lincoln,* was still upon my knee. I picked it up and read again the story of the profound spiritual experience that marked the last days of the great President's life. As blind men long for light, Lincoln groped after a fuller, sweeter, more satisfying faith. He tried many of the gates by which other pilgrims had entered the city; but, wistfully as he had approached them, he was compelled to turn away with a heavy heart and a sad shake of the head. Then, on the page lying open on my knee, I come upon this: "I have been reading the Beatitudes," Lincoln says to a friend, "and can at least claim *one* of the blessings therein unfolded. It is the blessing pronounced upon those who *hunger and thirst after righteousness.*"

I must have read these words just before my eyelids proved too heavy for me; and they wove themselves into the fabric of my dream. But now that I peruse them afresh, with my strange dream as a background, I see that the vision that came to me is true. There is a gate—the widest and most welcoming gate of all—by which those pilgrims may enter the City of Blessedness who, painfully conscious of their lack of grace, nevertheless long for grace as the hart panteth after the water-brooks.

CHAPTER V
THE QUALITY OF MERCY

GOD can forgive the passing sin of the hot heart but not the inherent sin of the cold. Even he has no mercy for the unmerciful.—*John Ruskin.*

GERARD was dead. They laid him out for his last resting-place. Under his linen they found a horse-hair shirt.

"Ah," cried the young monks, "behold, a saint!"

Under the hair-cloth they found a long thick tress of auburn hair.

The monks started and were horrified. In the midst of the confusion Jerome entered.

"Put ill construction on no act done by a brother which can be construed innocently," he said. "Who are you to judge such a man as this was?"—*The Cloister and the Hearth.*

> . . THY love
> Shall chant its own beatitudes
> After its own life-working. A child-kiss
> Set on thy sighing lips shall make thee glad;
> A poor man served by thee shall make thee rich;
> A sick man helped by thee shall make thee strong;
> Thou shalt be served thyself by every sense
> Of service which thou renderest.
>
> —*Elizabeth Barrett Browning.*

CHAPTER V

THE QUALITY OF MERCY

"Blessed are the merciful: for they shall obtain mercy."

I

I HAVE seen hundreds of rivers in my time, but there is one that I know intimately. I have followed its entire course. To this day, although the adventure lies far back across the years, I love to close my eyes and fancy myself back in New Zealand among the delicious solitudes that enfold the Fairy Pool. We were strolling—John Broadbanks and I—up among the grim and silent hills, when suddenly we caught that most satisfying and most melodious note that even nature ever strikes—the soft and silvery plash of water falling into water. Allured by the seductive call, we soon found ourselves in a thickly wooded dell adorned by a sort of natural grotto, over which the ferns climbed with prodigal luxuriance, while thick green mosses covered every stone. The song of the birds on all the branches about us blended perfectly with the music of the mountain spring. At the end of this lovely paradise, a gaily colored parrakeet sat on a low branch of the manuka, admiring his own image in the crystal bath below. And, just beyond him, was the spring which, gushing from a nest of mosses,

63

gurgled down a channel that it had worn for itself in the solid rock, to pour itself into the shining pool over which the bird was proudly perched. And the overflow of this mossy basin, trickling on down the valley, is the fountainhead of the river on which so many of our midsummer days were blissfully spent.

A little way down the hill other springs add their modest contributions to its volume. A mile or two further on it is a babbling stream in which you may watch the trout as, after flashing to and fro beside the bank, they conceal themselves under the turfy projections at the water's edge. A few miles further still, it is a pretty waterway on which holiday parties, in boats and canoes, dart in and out of the coves and gullies, admiring the graceful slopes on either side. Small settlements have sprung up here and there along its course, and a little steamer maintains a busy commerce between them. And then, in the spacious reaches with which we were more familiar, the current broadens out into a noble river, flanked by high hills all draped in virgin bush. And, right in front of the little cottage that served us as a holiday home, it emptied itself, amidst the roaring of the waters on the sandy bar, into the immensities of the blue, blue sea.

Somehow, the imagery of this glorious stream rushes to my mind as I set myself to explore the fifth beatitude. *"Blessed are the merciful: for they shall obtain mercy."* The mercifulness that gladdens the darkest corners of the earth, cheering the gloomiest hours of human existence, is like a clear and noble river flowing down from heights supernal, that it may fertilize, freshen, and beautify all climes, all civilizations, and all ages.

II

For mercifulness is essentially a Christian grace. Nobody can travel far without being impressed by the gulf that yawns, at this point, between the sentiments that prevail in a Christian country on the one hand and in heathen lands on the other. You may, of course, see the most revolting cruelty under the shadow of a church spire, and you may be treated with the most wonderful kindness amid pagan temples, but the general trend of things is in the opposite direction. In lands that have not as yet capitulated to the authority of the cross, there is very little respect for the feelings of animals. In a crowded Eastern bazaar I have seen a native woman sitting under the shade of a palm tree tearing a live fowl limb from limb, gloating with evident enjoyment over the hideous struggles of her writhing victim. Yet the crowd surged by unmoved, seeing nothing extraordinary and nothing deplorable in her horrible amusement. Travelers and missionaries tell such stories by the thousand.

The world would have been a pitiless place if Jesus had never entered it. It is, of course, sublimely true that millions of men and women who make no profession of Christianity perform deeds of mercy every day. That pleasing circumstance in no way affects the issue. It simply proves, as Miss Frances Power Cobbe used to say, that, as a result of fifty generations of Christianity, something of the spirit of Jesus has become ingrained in the very blood of the race, and it would take thousands of years of atheism to get it out again. But for the unconscious influence of Christ upon the lives of these merciful men, and upon their ancestors, they would never have seen any need to be kind, would never have included mercy among their cherished ideals, would never have felt within their breasts the urge of tender and compassionate instincts. Without knowing it, they are acting under the divine impulse of Christianity; they are following blindly and unwittingly in the footsteps of the Nazarene.

The idea of showing consideration or pity to a stranger or a foe never entered the world until Christianity emphasized the obligation; and it has only been found in the track of Christian apostles and teachers ever since. We can never forget that the neglect, exposure, and murder of new-born babes was a common practice throughout the world —even amid the philosophy of Rome and the culture of Greece—at the time when Christ appeared to show men a more excellent way. There is no trace of such an institution as a hospital prior to the dawn of the Christian era. And not one has ever been established since save under the direct or indirect influence of Christian teaching. Christlessness in any society means mercilessness. Rome, in the pomp of her glory, and in the climax of her culture, had for her chief amusement and delight the sanguinary combats between man and man, and between men and wild beasts, in the Colosseum. Rich and poor—with priests and vestal virgins among them—looked on approvingly, applauding tumultuously. Heathendom is pitifully destitute of that mercifulness which is so universally and eloquently manifested by the hospitals, orphanages, schools, asylums, almshouses, and similar institutions with which we are now so familiar. Such monuments mark the forward march across the nations of the Son of God.

Moreover, lands like our own are only beautified by exhibitions of mercy to the extent to which they have yielded to the Saviour's regal sway. The most Christian peoples are only superficially Christian: the relics of barbarism slumber just beneath the skin. Is it not significant that, even in lands like these, we should need such an organization as a Society for the Prevention of Cruelty to Animals, a Society for the Prevention of Cruelty to Children, and a Society for Relief of the Destitute Blind, and the like? The difficulty is, not to protect human beings from the ferocity of the beasts, but to protect dumb-driven cattle from the neglect, maltreatment, and cruelty of humans. Every such organization testifies at one and the same time to the mercifulness, begotten of Christian sympathy, which prompts its formation; and to the mercilessness of human nature when it is unaffected by, or has broken beyond the restraints of, Christian influence. The only mercifulness that is strong and steadfast and reliable is that which has come along the lines indicated in the Beatitudes. The heart that has been reduced to a beautiful poverty of spirit; the heart that has mourned in lowliest contrition; the heart that has learned the subtle secret of meekness; the heart that has hungered and thirsted after righteousness—such a heart is alone qualified to exhibit mercy in its tenderest and most effective forms.

III

And so it comes to pass that, just as it is easy to trace the flow of the river back to that mossy grotto in which the birds admire their plumage in the mirror of the Fairy Pool, so it is easy to trace the flow of the stream of human mercy back to its sublime fountainhead. It has its source in the very nature of God. Every merciful thought and purpose and intention existing in the minds of men is simply an evidence that God, being a perennial fountain of mercy, created man in his own likeness. Mercy is of the very essence of Deity.

Is it any wonder, then, that He who is the brightness of the Father's glory and the express image of his Person should crystallize the beauty of mercy into a pearl-like beatitude? It becomes those, he says, who are the subjects of mercy that is as wide as the world and as deep as the ocean to be merciful to one another. *"Freely ye have received; freely give"* is sound reasoning. *"Be ye kind one to another, tenderhearted, forgiving one another, even as God for Christ's sake hath forgiven you."* Jesus himself likens the merciless recipient of mercy to that wicked and unfaithful servant who, having been forgiven the ten thousand talents which he owed, nevertheless seized by the throat his fellow servant who owed him an hundred pence, and cried, "Pay me that thou owest!" *"O thou wicked servant! I forgave thee all that debt because thou desiredst me. Shouldst thou not also have had mercy on thy fellow servant, even as I had mercy on thee?"*

If the wonder of the eternal mercy is allowed to have its full effect upon us, it will melt these adamantine hearts of ours, so that we, whose trespasses have been so richly forgiven, will count it life's greatest luxury to forgive those who have at some time trespassed against us.

IV

Thinking of that lovely river as it winds its way down among the valleys, beautifying and immeasurably enriching the farms, the orchards, and the settlements along its banks, the memory somehow helps me to trace the flow of this other stream as it threads its course through a dusty, thirsty world. Its waters are wonderfully clear and translucent.

From their silvery surface to their tranquil depths, from their sacred source to their distant destiny, they are crystal clear: their transparent purity is a thing ineffable.

The animation of rivers renders them animate things; each possesses individuality and character; in some subtle way it conveys its own spirit to every landscape that it adorns. To secure the blessing of the fifth beatitude, every phase and feature of my life must be permeated by the sweetness of this beatific stream.

"Flow gently, sweet Afton!" I hear the words rising from a clear, fresh young voice in the opposite room. And, as I contemplate this other stream, I echo them. Flow gently—gently—so gently that every slightest movement of my mind may be infected by thy gentleness. The felicity of the fifth beatitude never takes up its abode in hearts that are quick to suspect, swift to condemn, slow to forgive. In thy gentle flow make all my *thoughts* merciful *thoughts!*

Flow smoothly, sweet Afton!—so smoothly that every word I utter shall partake of thine unruffled calm! No weapons can be more merciless than words. They can be more brutal than the most barbarous implements of torture ever devised by the malignant genius of a Grand Inquisitor. Tipped with ridicule, touched with scorn, steeped in irony, sharpened by sarcasm, a rasping tongue may shatter the peace of a household, inflicting wounds that will smart and sting and throb until death mercifully erases the ghastly phrases from the memory. That wretched man flings from him the priceless boon of this beatitude who yields to hasty, turbulent, passionate speech. Flow smoothly, beauteous stream; in thy serene flow make all my *words* merciful *words!*

Flow deeply, sweet Afton!—so deeply that the inmost springs of my being, the secret impulses of my soul, may be saturated in thy gracious and benignant temper! For, after all, it is the motive that matters. The mercifulness of Jesus consisted, not in healing the sick and curing the blind, but in having compassion on the multitude. The faces of the crowd went to his heart; he was touched with the feeling of their infirmities; their sorrows brought heaviness to his soul; and, when they wept, it brought tears to his eyes. The fifth beatitude breathes its blessing on sympathetic hearts and on spirits overflowing with human tenderness. Flow deeply, noble stream! May all my *motives* be merciful *motives;* all my *impulses* merciful *impulses!*

Flow mightily, sweet Afton!—so mightily that every outward deed of mine shall convey a recognition of thine influence upon me! In a world of aching and of breaking hearts, there is no room for harshness, for bitterness, for icy indifference. To serve men healingly and helpfully, I need, in all that I say and give and do, to leave the impression of vivid sympathy, of genuine affection, and of the sheer joy of serving. Flow mightily, glorious stream; in thy resistless flow make every *deed* of mine a compassionate, merciful *deed!*

V

Like the river on its way to the sea, the merciful man cherishes in his heart a sublime secret. The river is pouring itself out all the time; yet it grows as it flows; and, in its onward sweep, it rejoices in witnessing the freshening verdure of the adjacent fields and the increasing loveliness of the wild flowers that bespangle its banks. There is, as the merciful man well knows, *there is that scattereth and yet increaseth; and there is that withholdeth more than is meet, but it tendeth to poverty.* We have all been charmed by the story of Sir Launfal's search for the Holy Grail—the cup out of which Christ drank with his disciples at the Last Supper. The poet tells how Sir Launfal spent his whole life in the sacred pilgrimage. Then, when returning, old, weary, worn, and possessing but one last crust, he meets a leper, almost starved, who begs an alms "for Christ's sweet sake," Sir Launfal shares with him his crust and brings him water from the stream. Then, suddenly, the leper is no longer a leper, but the Crucified, and the cup from which he drinks is changed into the Holy Grail! In showing mercy to another he had found what he had so long and vainly sought. So blessedness, the Lord of the Beatitudes declares, consists in

". . . what we share,
For the gift without the giver is bare;
Who gives himself with his alms feeds three,
Himself, his hungry neighbor, and me."

It is very wonderful, yet it is true, that He who gave us the fifth beatitude accepts as a sacrificial service rendered to himself every cup of cold water that merciful hands extend to thirsty lips.

"And still wherever Mercy shares
Her bread with sorrow, want and sin,
And Love the beggar's feast prepares,
The Uninvited Guest comes in.

"Unheard, because our ears are dull,
Unseen, because our eyes are dim,
He walks our earth, the Wonderful,
And all good deeds are done to him."

And so the waters flow at last into the sea from whence they sprang. The trickling fountain at the Fairy Pool consisted of water that had originally come from the ocean. The sun had wooed it into the clouds; the clouds had distilled it over the hilltops; and the mountain torrents had borne it back once more to the sea. So this gracious and all-refreshing stream, having its rise in the Eternal, empties itself into the Eternal again. The divine mercy is its fountainhead; the divine mercy is its goal.

"Blessed are the merciful: for they shall obtain mercy." They are not merciful *in order* that they may obtain mercy. I like to fancy that these waters,

as they pour themselves down through the valleys, gladdening every pasture through which they pass, are not deliberately searching for the sea. They dumbly feel that they sprang from the infinite; they feel that they belong to the infinite and that they can never be quite at rest until they reach the infinite again. But it is not of *this* that they are thinking. They think only of their mission. It is theirs to give to the grass its greenness and to the trees their beauty. It is theirs to refresh the tired horses that are led at evening to the ford, the sheep that browse at the water's edge, and the cattle that stand among the reeds and rushes. And, busy with their lowly labor, they rush on and ever on, singing as they go. And their song would vibrate with a still blither note if they had any inkling of the joyous surprises awaiting them. For, to its amazement, the river discovers that although, all along its course, it is pouring itself out unselfishly and unstintingly, it nevertheless gets deeper and broader the farther it goes! This is the *first* astonishment, and the *second* is even more bewildering. For, one great day, as the waters turn a bend in the channel, they see, stretching out in its blue immensities, the infinite from which they sprang! So mercy greets mercy. *"Blessed are the merciful: for they shall obtain mercy."* The merciful, made merciful by mercy, find mercy in its fullness awaiting them at last.

CHAPTER VI
THE BEATIFIC VISION

ELDER sister, elder brother,
Come and go around the mother,
  As she bids them come and go:
But the babe in her embrace
Rests and gazes on her face,
  And is most happy so.

And oh! if earthly beauty beaming
From frail mother's face, rush streaming
  Deep into her infant's heart,
What rare beauty theirs must be,
Heavenly God, who gaze on thee!
  Who see thee as thou art!

—W. B. Robertson of Irvine.

GOLDILOCKS said a good thing on Sunday night. She was squatting on the hearthrug in her nightdress, learning the Beatitudes for her teacher.

"Well," I said, when she closed her Bible. "Which do you like best?"

"Oh, the sixth!" she replied at once.

"And why?"

"Because, if I were pure in heart, I should have all the other virtues as well!"—*John Broadbanks, of Silverstream, New Zealand.*

CHAPTER VI

THE BEATIFIC VISION

"Blessed are the pure in heart: for they shall see God."

I

"Blessed are the pure in heart: for they shall see God!" This shining beatitude stands out from the others as Mount Everest stands out from the Himalayas—snowcapped, sunlit, sublime. And yet, viewed from another angle, I sometimes fancy that, as beatitude followed beatitude, these golden epigrams grow less and less at variance with the ancient conception of happiness. This sixth, and most exacting of the series, sounds at first like an echo of the teaching of the earlier schools. Epicurus, the father of the Epicurean philosophy, taught, as his primary maxim, that happiness was the highest aim to which mortals could aspire, and that without virtue life could never be made really glad.

A more penetrating analysis, however, soon convinces us that the terms of the philosopher and of the Master were by no means synonymous. The *happiness* of Epicurus was as shallow as a dwindling, trickling stream at midsummer, compared with which the *blessedness* of which Christ speaks is as deep as the unfathomable sea. In the same way, between the *virtue* of the philosopher and the *purity*

77

in heart of Jesus, there is as much difference as exists between a skeleton and a living man, or between the faint shadow and the solid substance.

Still, the fact remains that the philosopher is right as far as he goes. The flimsy abstinence from gross immorality which he calls *virtue* does undoubtedly conduce to the shallow satisfaction that he calls *happiness*. But Jesus came to teach a richer and a sublimer truth. He speaks of *purity of heart*—a holier thing than philosophy ever dreamed of. He speaks of *seeing God*—a loftier rapture than philosophy ever aspired to. *The pure in heart,* he says, *shall see God.*

Two stupendous principles underlie this searching utterance. The *first* is that heart-purity is the essential condition to the reception of a divine revelation. God can reveal himself more readily to the pure in heart than to the mighty in intellect. The testimony of a little child who has learned to love God is, in spiritual matters, more to be trusted than the witness of gray-haired sages whose hearts are alienated from him. It is the pure-hearted Samuel who, while Eli slumbers, hears the voice divine. *"With the pure thou wilt show thyself pure." "The pure in heart shall see God."*

The *second* is that, in the spiritual life, there is a law of action and reaction constantly at work. Those who are pure in heart see God; the vision of the Eternal intensifies the purity of their hearts; and this again increases their desire and their capacity for fresh revelations. When a leak occurs in the famous dykes of Holland, the water rushes through the cavity with such tremendous force that it tears the opening larger and larger. The enlarging vacuum makes room for a greater rush of water, while the growing volume of water constantly expands the vacuum. The two processes act and react one upon the other. The leaves of the tree inhale vitality from the atmosphere, and thus minister to the life of the remotest roots. Simultaneously, the invigorated roots suck up the nutriment from the earth and communicate strength to the loftiest boughs. There is constant action and reaction. Every vision of God increases a Christian's hatred of sin and intensifies his struggle after holiness; while at every inch of progress in that divine path he gets a more radiant vision of the face of God.

This law of reaction proceeds unbroken until time melts into eternity. The pure in heart become purer and yet purer as the revelations of the divine become clearer and yet clearer, till at last, pure as God is pure, they stand in his insufferable presence and behold with seraphic rapture the beauty of his face. The blurred gaze of the impure, on the contrary, deepens into total blindness until, destitute of all moral perception and spiritual vision, they stagger tragically out into the everlasting dark.

II

"Blessed are the pure in heart!" The words fall

upon my ears like sweetest poetry and my conscience approves their perfect justice. Of course! Who but the pure in heart *should* be blessed? Who but the pure in heart *should* see God? And yet; and yet—! What if my heart be already sullied? What if it be already impure? The question suggests a parable. I looked upon the face of a little child, and, at first thought, I cried "Would to God I were as pure as he!" But I thought again, and, as this sixth beatitude whispered its soft, strong message to my soul, I thanked God that a finer, nobler purity than the purity of babyhood might be mine.

The difference is this: I saw a field in wintertime, and the earth looked wondrously free from weeds. But, stooping and brushing back the soil, I saw at every hand's touch the white and green blades of hundreds of weeds about to shoot through. That is the purity of babyhood. I saw the field again in summertime, and once more it was clean. But this time the turning back of the soil failed to discover any hidden growths. Having been plowed and turned, every malignant and destructive growth has been torn out.

That is the purity that may come to the heart of the vilest offender who truly believes. We cannot have the *first*—the purity of childhood—and we would not if we might; but we may have the *second* —the purity of redeemed manhood—and that is better, far. *This* is the balm that the sixth Beatitude affords to contrite hearts.

III

"Blessed are the pure in heart!" It is a choice utterance—and a terrible one. Its inwardness is revealed in its closing words: Blessed are the pure *in heart!* It is a great thing to be pure in *body,* pure in deed. It is a greater thing to be pure in *mind,* pure in thought and conception and fancy. But to be pure in *heart*—pure to the very source and center of one's secret being—pure as God is pure! The words appall me. I listen to this gemlike utterance and tremble. As an expert swordsman, by a dexterous lunge, can thrust his weapon home, converting into a fatal wound what might have been but a surface gash, so this Prince of Preachers, by the adroit and skillful turn given to his keen-edged words, pierces the hearts and consciences of his auditors with truths which, in other hands, might merely have elicited applause. Blessed are the poor *in spirit!* Blessed are the pure *in heart!*

Blessed are the pure! If the beatitude had ended there, every hearer would have endorsed and appreciated it. The Jews prided themselves on their ceremonial cleansings and purifications. But the pure *in heart!* Jesus knew the depths of humanity. The soul is often like the old Castle of Chillon on the fair lake of Geneva. The upper apartments were tastily decked out for the Duke of Savoy and his beautiful bride; while, in a lower dungeon, Bonnivard, the republican, lay for years in chains, his wretched existence made still more abominable by the hideous things that wriggled and darted out of the innumerable cracks and crevices around his loathsome cell. No such noisome chambers disfigure the souls of the recipients of the sixth benediction. They are pure from the center to the circumference—pure through and through.

IV

And yet, while this great saying terrifies me, it also comforts me.

"Blessed are the pure in heart!" The heart is the throne; and on the throne Purity must reign supreme. The will—so difficult to control—must yield unreserved allegiance to Purity's beneficent rule. The imagination—so hard to confine—must no longer deck the mind with its seductive pictures; it must bow to the lofty beauty of unsullied purity. The thoughts must be brought into absolute dominion; every purpose and intent must recognize the regal sway. Purity must reign in unquestioned authority.

All this may take time. The revolutionary and reactionary elements among my members cannot be subdued and subjugated in a single day. The flesh is mighty and does not readily capitulate; the fancy, accustomed to unfettered freedom, does not easily abandon its hectic flights. But there is all the difference in the world between that state of things in which the heart condones and secretly enjoys this waywardness and that state of things in which the heart forbids and deplores it.

"Lord, I believe: help thou mine unbelief!" cried one who recognized the simultaneous existence within his soul of faith and unbelief. But the essential point is that his central *ego,* his essential personality, his inmost heart associates itself with his faith and repudiates the unbelief. *I believe: help thou mine unbelief!* In the same way, the benediction of the sixth beatitude is breathed upon the man who, deploring the mutiny among his members, nevertheless cherishes in his heart the high ideal, the pure resolve. Every day of his life he cries on bended knees his fervid Litany: *"From all evil and mischief, from sin, from the crafts and assaults of the devil, by thine agony and bloody sweat, by thy cross and Passion, by thy precious death and burial, Good Lord, deliver me!"* And his Lord hears— and understands.

"Blessed are the pure in heart!" The heart is the fountainhead; and from that fountainhead the stream must proceed clear as crystal. It is no impossible ideal. There is no reason why life's vital stream should not gush clean and pure from *the heart* even though it become sullied later on. We often sneer at good intentions, forgetting that God is content to judge the intention while men judge only the resultant deed. The intention is by far the best criterion of the character. Thomas à Kempis found infinite comfort in the thought that

man considereth the deeds whilst God weigheth the intentions. Edith Cavell marked that sentence in her copy of the *Imitation* on that bleak October morning when she walked out to be shot. As some of our noblest rivers run sparklingly clean from their sources, only to be sullied and defiled further down, so a purpose may rise pure and sweet from the heart, and yet be marred by a forgetful mind or a clumsy hand. We may find consolation as well as condemnation in the declaration that the Lord seeth not as man seeth, for man looketh at the outward appearance, but the Lord looketh on *the heart.*

Plato was wont to compare the pure-hearted Socrates to the pottery of the apothecaries of Athens, on the *outside* of which were painted the ugly forms of apes and owls, while *within* were precious balms. And Lowell says that:

"We may hope that to our praise
    Our God not only reckons
The moments when we tread his ways,
    But when the spirit beckons—
That some slight good is also wrought
    Beyond self-satisfaction,
When we are simply good in thought,
    Howe'er we fail in action."

V

"Blessed are the pure in heart: for they shall see God." As a matter of fact, they have already seen him. In that fundamental fact lies the explanation

of their purity.   What is it that John Newton sings?

> "In evil long I took delight,
>   Unawed by shame or fear,
> Till a new object struck my sight,
>   And stopped my wild career."

And what was that sight that so strangely and suddenly arrested the downward course of the impious and dissolute sailor? Ask him. He says:

> "I saw One hanging on a tree,
>   In agonies and blood,
> Who fixed his languid eyes on me,
>   As near the cross I stood."

That sight struck him pure! The profligate, reeling before the mast of a slaveship, suddenly became a holy man, and was ere long an earnest and successful preacher of the gospel, the author of some of our most beautiful hymns, and a writer of enduring power! We have the same story in a different setting in the case of John Bunyan, and in the case of every truly pure man and woman who ever breathed. *"God, who commanded the light to shine out of darkness, hath shined into our hearts to give the light of the knowledge of the glory of God in the face of Jesus Christ."* They saw the wondrous glory in that wondrous Face, and the vision purified them. And, the revelation assuming even fresh vividness and splendor, their purity grows from more to more.

Yes, they have already seen God! That fact explains the attractiveness of the promise. Apart from it, the words are incomprehensible. Who that has never seen God desires to see him? Only those who have beheld the veiled beauty of that face have any strong desire to see it in its unveiled loveliness. Seeing that the objective revelation and the subjective purity act and react upon each other, it follows that only those in whom a partial revelation has already wrought *partial* purity have any fervent longing after the *complete* purity and the beatific vision. This was the thought that captivated the mind of Faber when he sang:

> "My God, how wonderful thou art,
>   Thy Majesty how bright!
> How beautiful thy mercy seat
>   In depths of burning light!
>
> "Father of Jesus, love's reward,
>   What rapture will it be
> Prostrate before thy throne to lie
>   And gaze and gaze on thee!"

VI

"Blessed are the pure in heart: for they shall see God." They *do* see him—see him every day. They behold the face of Deity at every turn. Nothing moves but they exclaim, "This is the finger of God!" Every sound is to them an echo of his voice. The very air is instinct with a sense of his gracious though invisible Presence. They see God in every

star that shines, in every flower that blooms, in every bird that sings, in every leaf that stirs.

" 'I come in little things,'
Saith the Lord:
'Yea, on the glancing wings
Of eager birds, and in brown bright eyes
That peep from out the brake, I stand confest
On every nest where feathery patience is content to brood,
And leaves her pleasure for the high emprise
Of motherhood,
There doth my Godhood rest.' "

The man who is pure in heart sees God in the imposing pageant of the past and in the wonders of today. His history books, his current magazines and newspapers are among his most practical commentaries on his Bible.

He sees God in all the affairs of life, in all its appointments—and its disappointments. He sees God in every means of grace. To him the Church is none other than the very house of God; to him every hymn is the outward expression of the inward gladness of a purified heart; to him the Word of God is ablaze with the glory of the Holiest, like the bush unconsumed in the midst of the flame. And, when he kneels in prayer, it seems to him that God is nearer to him than breathing, closer than hands or feet.

"Then, then on eagle wings he'll soar,
And time and space seem all no more;
Then heaven comes down his soul to greet
And glory crowns the mercy seat!"

Yes, beyond the shadow of a doubt, the pure in heart see God!

VII

"Blessed are the pure in heart: for they shall see God." They shall see him as they have never seen him yet. With open faces their pure spirits shall behold his glory. They shall see him, not in a beauteous dream or a brilliant flight of fancy, but vividly, clearly, constantly, forever and forever.

And so the benedictions of this beatitude pass ceaselessly through infinite processes of extension and expansion. Like shining atoms of quicksilver, they multiply themselves indefinitely. Blessed are the pure in heart, for they *have* seen God! Blessed are the pure in heart, for 'twas that sublime spectacle that made them pure! Blessed are the pure in heart, for they see God here and now! Blessed are the pure in heart, for that vision intensifies their purity! Blessed are the pure in heart, over and over and over again; blest with a blessedness that is perpetually augmenting and reproducing itself, and that will continue to do so until at last it finds its unspeakable, unthinkable consummation in the rapture of the supernal vision.

CHAPTER VII
THE OLIVE BRANCH

A PEACE is of the nature of a conquest;
For then both parties nobly are subdued,
And neither party loser.
      —Archbishop of York to Prince John in
      Shakespeare's *Henry the Fourth*.

LET it be that when our short day in this world is
over, and when the hour strikes for our going down
into the valley of the shadow, we may at least be able
to think that we have never said a word, nor thought
a thought which would dissociate the greatness of the
country of which we are proud to be citizens from the
cause of peace, which is also the cause of wisdom and
of strength.—*Lord Morley*.

IF you would preserve peace, then prepare for peace.
—*Barthelemy Prosper Enfantin*.

CHAPTER VII

THE OLIVE BRANCH

"Blessed are the peacemakers: for they shall be called the children of God."

I

FIRST pure; then peaceable, says James. *"The wisdom that is from above is first pure, then peaceable."* It is the divine order, and the Beatitudes follow it. *Blessed are the pure in heart! Blessed are the peacemakers!*

Blessed are the peacemakers! It was a war-sick world upon which the Saviour breathed this soothing benediction. The temple of Janus—the god of beginnings, from whose name we derive our word "January"—was erected in the reign of Numa Pompilius, seven hundred years before the angels sang of peace on earth at Bethlehem; and it was ordained that it was to be kept open in time of war and closed in time of peace. And only thrice—and then for the briefest possible periods—was it closed during all the seven centuries of its history. But a new day had dawned. The Babe whom the angels heralded in their *Gloria in excelsis* had come to still the clanging of human discords, to hush the hideous clash of bloodstained steel, and to lead the wayward and passionate hearts of men back to the paradise from which they had wandered. *Glory to God in the highest, and on earth peace!*

On earth peace! Blessed, he said, *are the peacemakers!* Thus he imposed his mission of reconciliation upon his Church. And the Church has retained her integrity and effectiveness only to the extent to which she has faithfully maintained that healing and pacifying ministry. Voltaire hated the Church, and he gave his reasons for his detestation. Prominent among his accusations stands the charge that the Church has failed at this very point. "Go through the five or six thousand sermons of Massillon," he says, "and you will scarcely find one in which a word is uttered against the scourge and crime of war. The same is true of Bourdaloue. Miserable physicians! Of what concern to me are benevolence, humanity, modesty, temperance, gentleness, wisdom, and piety so long as half an ounce of lead shatters my body and I die at twenty in torments unspeakable, surrounded by five or six thousand dead or dying, while my eyes, opening for the last time, see the town in which I was born delivered to fire and sword, and the last sounds that reach my ears are the shrieks of women and children expiring in the ruins—and the whole for the glory of some man whom I have never seen?" Whenever the Church forgets her mission, relaxing her efforts to win for herself the benediction of the peacemaker, she deserves to be castigated with some such stinging rebuke.

The theater of her opportunity is boundless, for the element of strife has entered into and permeated every department of life. It affects society in general. On every hand, in a million different forms, we meet rivalry, suspicion, and distrust. We see class contending with class; the rich oppressing the poor; the poor breathing maledictions on the rich. Petty jealousy mars the sweetness of every friendship; it stultifies the efficiency of every organization; and, entering our very churches, it disturbs and destroys that abiding unity that should be their most conspicuous charm.

It has a domestic bearing; for any violation of the spirit of this beatitude strips the beauty from every bride, and it nips the nobility of every bridegroom. It clouds the happy days of childhood with anger and bitterness. It sets husband against wife, father against son, mother against daughter. It finds its hideous memorial in the criminal and divorce courts, and shocks us in other ways equally revolting.

And who can contemplate the confusing tangles and the acrimonious jangles of the industrial world without recognizing that, in this direction, the Church has a sublime opportunity of creating a happier and healthier spirit?

II

Blessed are the peacemakers! By that pearl-like phrase the Saviour meant not so much men and women who will do a certain thing, as men and women who will display a certain spirit.

Blessed are the Perfume-makers!—He says, as he gazes on my garden. He does not mean that, by a frenzied effort, the rose is to pump forth fragrance. He knows that, if it be indeed a rose, it will exhale its sweet odor as an involuntary expression of its inner character. The peacemaker of the seventh beatitude is not a man who leaves his home every morning resolutely determined to reconcile and conciliate his fellow men. Such an attitude often produces a mere meddler and mischief-maker. The peacemaker of the seventh beatitude is a man whose very presence is a benediction. The spirit of peace wraps him about like an atmosphere; he exhales peace as a violet exhales sweetness; he breathes the very spirit of gentleness, geniality, and good will. It is impossible to spend five minutes in his company without feeling the better for it. You rise from a meal with him feeling as if you were leaving a communion table. In the course of a walk with him you remember the road to Emmaus. There is an unconscious influence about the true peacemaker that leads every man he meets to love his fellow men.

And there *are* such characters—souls that seem to walk the world on tiptoe. Their names are rarely in type; they are not shouting their orders among the leaders and commanders of the people; but quietly, serenely, tranquilly, like angels of peace, they move among those whose wounded spirits cherish a bitter resentment and whose hearts are hot with the lust for revenge. In the very approach of these gentle souls to such agitated sufferers there is something soothing; their accents fall on the ear with the assuaging effect of a balm. Their perfect poise and self-possession seem to say, as they cross each threshold, "Peace be to this house!" In their presence all tension vanishes; anger departs before the magic of their smile; their progress through life is an unconscious pilgrimage of healing. They do not lift up their voices and cry aloud; they do not scold or lecture or preach; the loom on which these peacemakers weave the web of peace makes not the slightest noise or fuss: these peacemakers do not even know that they are peacemakers; yet, under the soft breath of their charmed influence, swords become plowshares, spears are transformed into pruning hooks, the wilderness rejoices, and the desert blossoms as the rose.

III

There is a popular picture entitled "The Peacemaker." It represents a pair of sweethearts with whom the course of true love has run far from smoothly. They sit apart, their backs turned to each other. But, flitting to and fro between them, is a dainty little creature who, pleading with them to forget the silly trifle that has shattered so much felicity, urges them to kiss and be friends. We need such intervening angels—those who, with wondrous grace and skill and tact, know how to restore amity and friendship to lives that, to their own sorrow, have drifted asunder.

It is a delicate task and can only be undertaken by deft and skillful workmen. There are repairs that can be effected with needle and thread; there are repairs that can be effected with hammer and gimlet and saw; but there are repairs that can only be effected with honest looks, warm handclasps, tactful words, and understanding hearts. Only a soul that has traversed in tears and glory all the winding ways of these Beatitudes can successfully undertake such an enterprise. You are dealing with threads as fine as gossamer; you need the tenderness of an angel's touch and the unspoiled spirit of a little child. The seventh beatitude comprehends all that is expressed in the picture; but it comprehends more.

For the ideal peacemaker is the man who prevents the peace from being broken. To prevent a battle is the best way of winning a battle.

"I have heard," I once said to a Jewish rabbi, "I have heard that, at a Jewish wedding, a wineglass is broken as part of the symbolism of the ceremony. Is that a fact?"

"Of course it is," he replied. "We hold aloft a wineglass; let it fall and be shivered to atoms; and then, pointing to its fragments, we exhort the young people jealously to guard the sacred relationship into which they have entered, since, once it is fractured, it can never be restored."

The peacemaker is a *lover* of peace. He is wounded by the wounds of others. The sounds of strife and discord are an agony to his spirit. Lord Lucius Falkland is described by historians as the most chivalrous figure in English history. It was his misfortune to live in days of civil war, and, by letting men see that the horror of the conflict was eating into his very heart, he did much to bring hostilities to a close. "When," says Lord Clarendon, "when there was any overture or hope of peace, he would be more erect and vigorous, and exceedingly solicitous to press anything which he thought might promote it, and, sitting among his friends, often after a deep silence and frequent sighs, would, with a shrill and sad accent, ingeminate the word 'Peace! Peace!' and would passionately profess that the very agony of the war took his sleep from him, and would shortly break his heart and hurry him to his grave." It did. He died, like his Lord, at the age of thirty-three, and all who remembered him cherished, as long as they lived, a secret loathing of war and a resolve to keep the peace of England inviolate. It is such men—knightly souls with whom peace is a passion and war a nightmare—who exhale a fragrance and create an atmosphere in which strife and discord are impossible.

The peacemaker of whom the Saviour was thinking when he uttered the beatitude is a man who will take infinite pains to *give* no offense, by thought or word or deed, even to the most sensitive and susceptible. He will suffer in silence rather than, by *taking* offense, strain the relationship between some other and himself. And he will do everything in his power to exercise a healing and soothing influence in a world of discord and strife. *First-party* peacemaking—abstinence, that is, from *giving* offense—is the easiest form of peacemaking, and the best. *Second-party* peacemaking—abstinence, that is, from *taking* offense—is the next easiest and the next best. *Third-party* peacemaking—the intervention, that is, of a disinterested person—is at once the most difficult and least satisfactory; but it is possible, and, when occasion offers, the venture must be made.

IV

"Blessed are the peacemakers: for they shall be called the children of God." It is a striking guerdon. It is not that they shall *become* the children of God; they are *that* already; but they shall be *called* the sons of God. It is not a question of their identity but of their identification. The world will see it in their characters, their faces, their words, their deeds. And this will be the title that even the world will confer upon the peacemakers; it will call them sons of God. The idea is a very simple and a very familiar one. We meet a young fellow in the street. All at once, some little mannerism, some inflection of the voice, some movement of the hand, some expression of the face, recalls the memory of an old

friend. Is it possible? Is this his son? We inquire, and quickly find that our suspicion is well founded. That is precisely the idea of the seventh beatitude. The world will see in the peacemaker a softened, hallowed mirroring of the divine glory. "He gives offense to none, even when fiercely provoked," men will say; "he takes offense from none, even when directly insulted; he seeks to heal all wounded hearts about him. This is godlike; it is divine! He must be none other than a son of God!" The world will see the august descent of the peacemaker in the beautiful and tranquil sublimity of his spirit.

In such an one the world recognizes a striking likeness to *the* Son of God. "We saw a Peacemaker once before," the world will say. "We remember him as One who went about, not merely saying, 'Peace be to this house!' but actually conferring peace on every home he entered; we remember him as One who, living, said: *'My peace I give unto you!'* and, dying, bequeathed that peace to his disciples as a priceless legacy; we remember him as One whose advent into the world was heralded with angel songs of peace on earth and of good will toward men, and whose death was undertaken that he might make peace by the blood of his cross. Remembering *him*, we feel that this new peacemaker of our acquaintance must be related to him; he has the same nature, the same griefs, the same delights, the same characteristics; he must be, like him, a son of God."

This is the blessedness of the peacemaker. He has no need to tell men that he is a Christian. They tell him, what he himself sometimes doubts, that he is directly related to the Prince of Peace. They take knowledge of him that he has been with Jesus. *"Blessed are the peacemakers: for they shall be called the sons of God."*

Am I conscious of having broken the peace with any man? I must go at once, if I would receive this blessedness, and crave his forgiveness. Am I conscious of having been injured or offended? I must go to my friend, tell him how deeply I regret the breach, and clasp his familiar hand once more. Hard, is it? So was the cross; but that was the only way in which the Prince of Peacemakers could make peace. The materials out of which he fashioned the everlasting peace were two rude blocks of wood and a handful of nails. His followers must be dismayed by no difficulty or sacrifice short of Gethsemane and Calvary.

I may be comforted by the assurance that, whether my errand succeed or fail, I have earned the title of peacemaker; I have shown myself a child of God; I have secured for my soul the blessedness of this beatitude. Even should my effort fail, my peace will return to me. If I have not succeeded in making peace with another, I have at least secured a greater peace for my own heart. Unless I make some honest attempt at conciliation, there must always remain a blessedness above and beyond me which my soul has never tasted and my heart never known.

It is up to this lofty altitude, with its rarified atmosphere, that all the beatitudes have led. Make peace; make peace! And, with all your peacemaking, make peace with God. Without *this,* all other peace is hollow, valueless, and hardly worth the making. But peace having been made with God, that *major* peace will shine like a golden haze about all our *minor* peacemaking. For, as the glowing words put it, *he* is our peace, and, through *him,* we both have access by one spirit—the peace-spirit—unto the Father.

CHAPTER VIII

THE MARTYR'S CROWN

I HAVE borne scorn and hatred,
　I have borne wrong and shame,
Earth's proud ones have reproached me
　For Christ's thrice blessèd name.
Where God his seal set fairest
　They've stamped their foulest brand;
But judgment shines like noonday
　In Immanuel's land.

They've summoned me before them,
　But there I may not come.
My Lord says, "Come up hither,"
　My Lord says, "Welcome Home!"
My kingly King, at his white throne,
　My presence doth command,
Where glory—glory dwelleth
　In Immanuel's land.

—*Mrs. A. R. Cousin's Paraphrase of the last
words of Samuel Rutherford.*

WHEN we shall live in that Day, we shall look with
wonder on one another, and say, "Shame, that we were
not of better cheer, braver, stronger, and more joyful,
to trust Christ and to endure all tribulations and crosses
and persecutions, since this glory is so great."—*Martin
Luther.*

FOR all thy saints who from their labors rest,
Who thee by faith before the world confessed,
Thy name, O Jesus, be forever blest.
　　　　　Halleluia!

O may thy soldiers, faithful, true and bold,
Fight as the saints who nobly fought of old,
And win with them the victor's crown of gold!
　　　　　Halleluia!

—*W. W. How.*

CHAPTER VIII

THE MARTYR'S CROWN

"Blessed are they which are persecuted for righteousness' sake: for theirs is the kingdom of heaven.

"Blessed are ye, when men shall revile you, and persecute you, and shall say all manner of evil against you falsely, for my sake.

"Rejoice and be exceeding glad: for great is your reward in heaven: for so persecuted they the prophets which were before you."

I

THE eighth beatitude is a postscript, a supplement, an afterthought. *"Blessed are they which are persecuted for righteousness' sake."* Unlike its predecessors, it deals, not with some definite phase of the happy man's character, but with the treatment that he receives at the hands of an unsympathetic, unappreciative, and hostile world. And yet, just as it is said that the best part of certain letters is to be found in the postscript, so, in the judgment of the Church's most saintly and seraphic teachers, this is the climax and crown of the Beatitudes, the highest note in the octave. When Saint Francis de Sales was asked which of the eight he preferred, he chose this one; and, when pressed for his reason, replied: "Because it shows that the disciples are as their Lord; their life is hid with Christ in God; they are conformed to his image and likeness; for, all through his earthly life, *he* was persecuted for the sake of that very righteousness which he came to fulfill."

"Blessed are they which are persecuted for righteousness' sake!" As he uttered these priceless Beatitudes, the Master stood among the three great hosts of whom we sing in the *Te Deum*. Behind him, in the dim perspective of history, stood the Goodly Fellowship of the Prophets; he was immediately surrounded by the Glorious Company of the Apostles; and, looking down the ages, he surveyed the Noble Army of Martyrs. But he had them *all* in mind when he uttered this concluding benediction. The prophets were sawn asunder; the apostles were stoned and burned; their great Lord and Leader himself was nailed to the bitter tree; yet in every case a fountain of blessedness, welling up within, triumphed over the turbulent curses that raged without.

Indeed, he had his whole Church in mind—the Church of all times and of all climes. For the eighth beatitude includes us all. It would be a thousand pities to confine its scope to those heroes of the faith whose names are writ large in Master Foxe's famous volume.

Every Christian worth his salt has suffered persecution. I like to think that, fearful lest some of us should feel ourselves excluded from this final blessing, the Master went out of his way to amplify its scope and define its terms. "Blessed are *ye*," he added, dividing persecution into *three* distinct classifications, "blessed are ye when men shall revile you, persecute you, and say all manner of evil against you falsely for my sake." Paul adheres to the same threefold division in writing to the Corinthians: "Being *reviled,* we bless; being *persecuted,* we suffer it; being *defamed* we entreat." One or other of these words leads every true Christian who ever lived into the felicity of the last beatitude. At some time or other he has probably been actually *persecuted.* He has been harassed, annoyed, tormented, involved in some severe penalty or subjected to some disability for his Saviour's sake. Or he has been *reviled*—affronted to his face; openly snubbed, insulted, or jeered at. Or at least he has been *defamed.* Behind his back men have said all manner of evil against him, falsely.

Nero was fond of dressing the early Christians in the skins of sheep and of bears, and, having thus attired them, he baited them with dogs, as though they were sheep and bears indeed. The grotesque custom has not altogether gone out of favor yet. It is a comparatively common thing to speak evil of a good man, and then treat him as if he were as evil as the venomous scandal suggests. The man who has resolutely laid to heart the message of this last beatitude will be undismayed by all such defamation. He knows that you may beat and batter the genuine coin of the realm as you will; you may cover it with filth and contamination to your heart's content; you cannot degrade its own inherent worth; it will be recognized at the mint; and, melted down, its metal will glow in mirror-like purity once more.

"Blessed are they that are persecuted for righteousness' sake: for theirs is the kingdom of heaven."

II

Blessed are the persecuted! At first blush the words appear like a paradox. How can pain be pleasant? How can torture be felicitous? And yet, on second thoughts, they seem more like a truism. The persecuted happy? Of course they are happy! In *Middlemarch*, George Eliot has a striking passage in which she declares that the spiritual genius of Bunyan never reveals itself more tellingly than in his description of the trial of Faithful. In their malice and ferocity, the persecuting passions bring in their verdict of Guilty: yet who pities Faithful? He is the one sublime, unconquerable, altogether enviable figure in the dramatic scene. "That," says George Eliot, "is a rare and blessed lot, which some of the greatest men have not attained, to know ourselves guiltless before a condemning crowd—to be sure that what we are denounced for is solely the good in us." And she adds that no man is more to be pitied than the man who, being tormented, realizes that he is suffering, not for righteousness' sake, but for not being the man he pretended to be! The martyrology of the Church sounds like some full-voiced paean, some noble anthem, some glorious oratorio. The men who have suffered have been the men who have sung.

The persecuted are blessed by reason of the factors that led to their persecution. They have been permitted to see truth to which other eyes were blind. They have been like those snow-capped summits that, because of their altitude and purity, are first to catch the crimson flush of dawn. It is one of the striking facts of history that, wherever men have sought sincerely after truth, the truth has been revealed to them. And, having found the pearl for which they sought, they have paid the price with a smile. In the secrecy of their souls they have heard voices which seemed to convey to them the congratulations of highest heaven. *"Blessed,"* exclaimed those voices, *"blessed are the eyes which see the things that ye see; for I tell you that many prophets and kings have desired to see those things which ye see, and have not seen them; and to hear those things which ye hear, and have not heard them."* Every martyr, ancient and modern, has rejoiced in the truth that led him to suffer, and would ten thousand times rather possess that truth and die in torture, than live, either never having seen it, or having seen and betrayed it. In view of the wealth of the spiritual treasury which has been entrusted to him, he smiles at the stake, hurls defiance at death, and greets the unseen with a cheer.

He feels too a thrill of exultation at the thought of the company he keeps. His sufferings identify him with an exalted and triumphant brotherhood. "If," said the Master, under the shadow of the cross, *"if ye were of the world, the world would love its own, but because ye are not of the world, therefore the world hateth you. If they have persecuted me, they will also persecute you."* The man who goes without the camp bearing the reproach of the cross, shares the fellowship of his Saviour's sufferings and experiences the joy of identification with him. Persecution is the world's testimony to the Church's purity. A wolf will not worry a painted sheep; a cat will not seize a toy mouse. The world may despise, but it will not persecute, a counterfeit Christian; it may scorn, but it will not burn, a hypocrite. Crucifixion is the evidence of Christliness.

III

Blessed are the persecuted! They are happy in respect of the joys that accompany their sufferings. "Surely," exclaimed John Bradford, as they bound him to the stake, "surely if there be any way to heaven on horseback, it is by the cross!" The man who endures persecution for the truth's sake is supported by the applause of his own conscience. He knows that his cause is right, and that, in the end, the truth for which he suffers must prevail. Even pagan philosophers felt the force of such reasoning.

"Keep your divinity pure," says Marcus Aurelius, the Imperial Stoic. "Cleave to the right. Be true to the best in yourself. Fear nothing and regret nothing. Stand boldly for the truth of your testimony. Then, come what may, you will be happy: the whole world cannot cheat you of your conquest." The man who stands true to truth will find that truth will stand true to him; wisdom will be justified of all her children.

In the consciousness of heavenly honor, the martyrs have welcomed earthly shame; in the knowledge of divine coronation, they have endured human crucifixion. *"Fear not,"* they have heard a voice say to them, *"fear not, for . . . when thou passest through the waters, I will be with thee; and through the rivers, they shall not overflow thee; when thou walkest through the fire, thou shalt not be burned; neither shall the flame kindle upon thee."*

That is the passage marked in the Bible of Thomas Bilney, which may still be seen at Corpus Christi College, Cambridge. He marked it while he was awaiting the fiery ordeal amidst which his radiant spirit subsequently took its flight. That promised presence has been vividly experienced by all who have endured hardship for the Saviour's sake. The form like unto the Son of God—the form that Nebuchadnezzar saw in attendance upon the three Hebrew children in the burning fiery furnace—was not more real to them, and was hardly more manifest to others, than that Presence has always been, in similar circumstances, all down the ages.

However it may be explained, the indisputable fact remains that the annals of martyrdom represent a story of ecstasy, a drama of exultation, a pageant of rapturous triumph. Men seemed, as Lecky finely says, to have fallen in love with death. Beyond the shadow of a doubt, the sentiment of this beatitude has been verified by the acid test of actual experience. The persecuted have been men of burning hearts and shining faces. Criminals and other unfortunates, confronted by a cruel ordeal at the last, have died calmly, stoically, philosophically. But that is not the distinguishing feature of the deaths of the martyrs. They met their deaths not only with resignation and with courage, but joyously, ecstatically, gloriously. The face of Stephen was as it were the face of an angel; and the celestial experience of that first Christian martyr has been repeated in hundreds of thousands of cases since. The joy of the martyrs was the force that surprised and convinced thousands of spectators in the early persecutions in the Roman Empire. Men were amazed to see the Christians going out to die, their faces aglow with triumph and with songs upon their lips.

The later persecutions bear the same hallmark. The first martyrs in the cause of the Reformation marched into the fire singing praise to God. The Covenanters of Scotland met death in the same way;

while time would fail to recite the illustrious names of those who sang amid the flames on English soil. The same story has been repeated in our own time. The persecuted Christians of Madagascar sang hymns of adoration even when oppressed with the most barbarous cruelties. Bishop Hannington marched to his death at Uganda singing "Safe in the arms of Jesus," and his successor, Bishop Tucker, in ordaining a native of Uganda to the Christian ministry, said of him: "This remarkable man has been beaten, imprisoned, put in the chain gang, had his house burned down and all his property destroyed; yet he has borne it all with a smile upon his face and a song upon his lips." It is the same all the ages through. Even in the midst of the most excruciating sufferings, the felicity promised by the last beatitude never fails.

IV

Blessed are the persecuted! They are blessed by reason of the benefits which flow from their persecution. If it were possible to compile a statement showing the extent to which the martyrs have enriched the world, it would be one of the most striking contributions to our literature. Their sturdy characters, their magnificent testimonies, their exalted principles, their heroic deaths—these are items in our annals for which the world must ever be grateful. They inspire in us a contempt for mere material comfort: they impress us with the sublimity and preciousness of things unseen. And, in the great majority of cases, we should have known nothing of these men, of their principles, or of their sterling worth, but for their persecution. They would have preached to their dozens, their scores, or their hundreds. The hand of the persecutor has sought to stifle their voices, and has succeeded, instead, in amplifying those voices indefinitely. He has exalted the lowly preacher to a pulpit of fire, sending his teachings ringing across wide empires and echoing down the ages. Latimer and Ridley testified by their lives to their own day and generation; but Latimer spake but the barest truth when, at the stake, he said to his companion, "Be of good cheer, Master Ridley, for by the grace of God we shall light such a candle in England today as shall never be put out!"

> "In Oxford town the faggots they piled,
> In furious haste and with curses wild,
> Round two brave men of our British breed
> Who dared to stand true to their speech and deed.
> Round two brave men of that sturdy race,
> Who with tremorless souls the worst can face;
> Round two brave souls who could keep their tryst,
> Through a pathway of fire to follow Christ.
> And the flames leaped up, but the blinding smoke
> Could not the soul of Hugh Latimer choke;
> For, said he, 'Brother Ridley, be of good cheer,
> A candle in England is lighted here,
> Which by grace of God shall never go out,'
> And that speech in whispers was echoed about—
> *"Latimer's light shall never go out,*
> *However the winds may blow it about:*

Latimer's light has come to stay,
Till the trump of a coming Judgment Day!"

So true is it that the blood of the martyrs is the seed of the Church. And not only so. It is the constant and abiding inspiration of the Church. Here, for instance, is a young man. In the hour of temptation, he yields a sacred principle. He suddenly remembers that for that same principle his forefathers bled; and, blushing, he recoils from the allurement and plays the man. Here is a young woman. She was inclined to forsake the courts of the Lord's house, and her face was only occasionally seen in the sanctuary. She remembers that, in order to secure to her the inestimable privilege of worshiping God according to her conscience, the noblest spirits of all time have laid down their lives by the score; and, as a consequence of that reflection, the congregation sees her oftener now.

"Speak, History! Who are life's victors?
  Unroll thy long annals and say—
  Are they those whom the world calls the victors who won the
    success of a day?
  The Martyrs or Nero—the Spartans who fell at Ther-
    mopylae's tryst,
  Or the Persians and Xerxes?—his judges or Socrates?—
    Pilate or Christ?"

To that question there can be but one answer. History and experience agree in giving it. And, in giving it, they can find no language better suited to their purpose than the language of the eighth beatitude.

CPSIA information can be obtained at www.ICGtesting.com
Printed in the USA
BVOW06s1825070816

458165BV00011B/236/P